Sonic Encounters

Sonic Encounters

The Islamic Call to Prayer

Diana Chester

ROWMAN & LITTLEFIELD
Lanham • Boulder • New York • London

Credits and acknowledgments for material borrowed from other sources, and reproduced with permission, appear on the appropriate page within the text.

Published by Rowman & Littlefield
An imprint of The Rowman & Littlefield Publishing Group, Inc.
4501 Forbes Boulevard, Suite 200, Lanham, Maryland 20706
www.rowman.com

Copyright © 2021 by Diana Chester

All rights reserved. No part of this book may be reproduced in any form or by any electronic or mechanical means, including information storage and retrieval systems, without written permission from the publisher, except by a reviewer who may quote passages in a review.

British Library Cataloguing in Publication Information Available

Library of Congress Cataloging-in-Publication Data

Names: Chester, Diana, 1982– author.
Title: Sonic encounters : the Islamic call to prayer / Diana Chester.
Description: Lanham, Maryland : Rowman & Littlefield, [2021] | Includes bibliographical references and index. | Summary: "This book uses a sound studies framework to explore artistic research methods and practices in ethnography as they relate to religious recitation"—Provided by publisher.
Identifiers: LCCN 2021032792 (print) | LCCN 2021032793 (ebook) | ISBN 9781538160725 (cloth) | ISBN 9781538164082 (paperback) | ISBN 9781538160732 (epub)
Subjects: LCSH: Adhan. | Prayer—Islam.
Classification: LCC BP184.3 .C44 2021 (print) | LCC BP184.3 (ebook) | DDC 297.3/822—dc23
LC record available at https://lccn.loc.gov/2021032792
LC ebook record available at https://lccn.loc.gov/2021032793

*To the Next Generation
Ella, Lily, and Quinn*

OOO

Let the Adventures Begin

Contents

List of Figures		ix
List of Recordings		xi
Acknowledgments		xiii
Note		xv
Introduction		xvii
1	Recording Sound in Context: Soundmapping	1
2	Dahab, Egypt, 2003	7
3	Mosque Alarm Clock: Abu Dhabi, United Arab Emirates, 2011	11
4	Sounding the Adhan	15
5	Old Fish Market, Abu Dhabi, United Arab Emirates, 2010	21
6	Reykjavik, Iceland, 2017	29
7	A Method for Recording	37
8	Florence, Italy, 2017	43
9	Christchurch, New Zealand, 2019	51
10	Recording as Translation	55
11	Yangon, Myanmar, 2014	61
12	Bali, Indonesia, 2017	67
13	Sound as Memory	77

14	Al Dabb'iya, United Arab Emirates, 2014	83
15	Copenhagen, Denmark, 2017	89
16	Making Scholarly Art	99
17	Ezhara Beach, India, 2015	105
18	Protestors for Us: Sarasota, Florida, United States, 2016	111
19	The Sonic Context	123
20	Bangalore, India, 2010	129
21	Stockholm, Sweden, 2017	139
22	Ethnography and the Sonic Frame	147
23	Singapore, 2014	157
24	Madha, Oman, 2016	163

Conclusion	177
Endnotes	181
Bibliography	185
Index	187
About the Author	195

List of Figures

All pictures were taken by the author unless otherwise stated in respective chapters.

Figure I.1	Moslem Mosque Inc. (MMI) Brooklyn, New York, United States	xx
Figure 1.1	Soundmap of the Islamic Call to Prayer	3
Figure 3.1	Mosque Alarm Clock, United Arab Emirates	13
Figure 4.1	Tightmarte Village, Morocco	16
Figure 4.2	Akuafo Hall Mosque, University of Ghana Legon, Accra, Ghana	18
Figure 5.1	Sheikh Khalifa Mosque, Abu Dhabi, United Arab Emirates	22
Figure 5.2	W2 Mosque, Old Fish Market Megablock, Abu Dhabi, United Arab Emirates	26
Figure 6.1	Prayer Room in the Félag Múslima Á Íslandi, Iceland	33
Figure 8.1	Masjid Al-Taqwa, Florence, Italy	49
Figure 9.1	Perth Mosque, Australia	52
Figure 9.2	Al Noor Mosque, Christchurch, New Zealand	53
Figure 10.1	Centro Cultural Beneficente Islâmico do Ceará, Fortaleza, Brazil	58
Figure 11.1	Chulia Muslim Dargah Mosque, Yangon, Myanmar	65
Figure 12.1	Ubudiyah Foundation Building Mushollah, Bali, Indonesia	72
Figure 13.1	Masjid Talha bin Obaidullah, Al-Ain Al-Baida, Jordan	81
Figure 15.1	Imam Ali Moskeen, Copenhagen, Denmark	96
Figure 17.1	Mosque in Ezhara Beach, Kerala, India	109
Figure 18.1	Islamic Society of Sarasota and Bradenton, United States	118

Figure 18.2	Members of Action Together Suncoast (ATS) Holding Signs, United States	120
Figure 20.1	Masjid E Noor, Bangalore, India	137
Figure 21.1	Islamiska Förbundet Stockholms Moské, Stockholm, Sweden	145
Figure 22.1	Al-Masjid An-Nabawi, Medina, Kingdom of Saudi Arabia	150
Figure 22.2	Salah Al-Deens Mosque Near Mt. Nebo, Jordan	152
Figure 23.1	Masjid Sultan, Singapore	160
Figure 24.1	Masjid Mushayhitan, Madha, Oman	176

List of Recordings

All field recordings in this list were made by the author unless otherwise stated in respective chapters.

Recording #0	Book Cover, Abu Darwish Mosque, Amman, Jordan	xvi
Recording #1	Moslem Mosque Inc. (MMI) Brooklyn, New York, United States	xx
Recording #2	Mosque Jebel Akhdar, Oman—Asr Adhan	5
Recording #3	Mosque Alarm Clock, Abu Dhabi, United Arab Emirates	13
Recording #4	Tightmarte Village, Morocco, Example of Tartīl Style of Recitation	17
Recording #5	Akuafo Hall Mosque, University of Ghana Legon, Accra, Ghana, Example of Tajwīd Style of Recitation	18
Recording #6	Sheikh Khalifa Mosque, Abu Dhabi, United Arab Emirates	23
Recording #7	W2 Mosque, Abu Dhabi, United Arab Emirates	26
Recording #8	Félag Múslima Á Íslandi, Reykjavik, Iceland	33
Recording #9	Masjid As-Sunnah An-Nabawiyyah, Philadelphia, Pennsylvania, United States	40
Recording #10	Masjid Al-Taqwa, Florence, Italy—Jumu'ah Adhan	50
Recording #11	Perth Mosque, Australia—Dhuhr Adhan	53
Recording #12	Al Noor Mosque, Christchurch, New Zealand—Dhuhr Adhan	54
Recording #13	Centro Cultural Beneficente Islâmico do Ceará, Fortaleza, Brazil	58

Recording #14	Chulia Muslim Dargah Mosque, Yangon, Myanmar	66
Recording #15	Ubudiyah Foundation Building Mushollah, Bali, Indonesia—Dhuhr Adhan	73
Recording #16	Masjid Talha bin Obaidullah, Al-Ain Al-Baida, Jordan	81
Recording #17	Sheikh Mubarak bin Mohammed Mosque, Al Dabb'iya, United Arab Emirates—Asr Adhan	87
Recording #18	Imam Ali Mosque, Copenhagen, Denmark—Dhuhr Adhan	96
Recording #19	Mosque in Ezhara Beach, Kerala, India	110
Recording #20	Islamic Society of Sarasota and Bradenton, United States—Jumu'ah Prayer	118
Recording #21	Masjid E Noor, Bangalore, India—Maghrib Adhan	137
Recording #22	Islamiska Förbundet Stockholms Moské, Stockholm, Sweden	145
Recording #23	King Hussein Mosque, Amman, Jordan	148
Recording #24	Al-Masjid An-Nabawi, Medina, Kingdom of Saudi Arabia—Isha'a Adhan	151
Recording #25	Salah Al-Deens Mosque near Mt. Nebo, Jordan—Dhuhr Adhan	153
Recording #26	Masjid Sultan, Singapore	161
Recording #27	Masjid Mushayhitan, Madha, Oman—Asr Adhan	176

MAP

Website	Soundmap of the Islamic Call to Prayer	3

Acknowledgments

It has taken ten years to research and write this book, and it has taken on a variety of shapes over that time. I received help, guidance, and support from many people along the way. I have to give the greatest thanks to the people in the communities I visited and wrote about, who welcomed me into their mosques, spoke with me about their communities, and allowed me to record their voices. This book is preceded by the Soundmap of the Islamic Call to Prayer, which contains a broader set of recordings of the adhan. I am grateful to all of the people who have helped to grow the soundmap over the years, those who have themselves made recordings, and those who have gotten others involved. The wider collection of recordings on the soundmap speak more cohesively to the extent of the research project out of which this book was born.

There are a number of people who have helped to further my thinking on this subject and have given support throughout the project in many forms, including critical feedback on writing, discussing Islam, and encouraging me to push forward when I was stuck. I would like to especially thank Stephanie Hopkins, Heidi Stalla, Jac Duran, Waseem Ahmed Allimia, and Maggie Bavuso. A big thanks to Imam Ismaeel Malik for his kindness and enthusiasm for this project as well as his contribution to chapter 6 "Reykjavik, Iceland, 2017" on the Félag Múslima Á Íslandi in Reykjavik, Iceland. A big thanks to Omer "Kashmir" Ahmed for his ongoing support with this project and written contribution to chapter 22 "Ethnography and the Sonic Frame," Guilherme Menezes for his contributions to the soundmap and written contribution to chapter 10 "Recording as Translation," and a big thanks to Kasey Kozara for her friendship and written contribution to chapter 15 "Copenhagen, Denmark, 2017." I want to thank Seersa Abaza for allowing me to use her image as my cover photo for the book.

I would also like to thank all of those who accompanied me on visits to mosques, who spent the time to talk to me about the project, and who allowed me to record their voices. While there are too many to name and those whose names I never learned, I would like to thank Anna Dechert, Ann Jyothis Raj, Robin Hemley, Chandan Nallal, Nischal Rao, Lauren Seaman, Dhanaraj Keezhara, Nisha Raj, Guðrún Guðmundsdóttir, Marcia Petersen, Michael Caponegro, Jack Sedorowitz, Brother Oli Halldorsson, Alyssa Haughwout, Renji Jacob, Ness Wild, and the Moslem Mosque Inc.

Financial support that made this book possible includes research funding from New York University Abu Dhabi, a Post-Doctoral Fellowship from Yale-NUS College that supported much of the writing, and support from the University of Sydney.

I am grateful to my family for their ongoing support and love. I want to especially thank my father, who throughout this process has delved into his own childhood to help me understand my Islamic heritage, and accompanied me to his family mosque in Brooklyn, New York, after a fifty-year hiatus. And my mother who has supported and encouraged my globe-trotting spirit from that first trip to Paris.

Sonic Encounters: The Islamic Call to Prayer is in part the result of PhD work completed at the University of Porto under the guidance of Rui Penha and Sarah Weiss, both of whose scholarship, mentorship, and kindness I am grateful for.

Note

All of the case studies in this book are factual accounts of my visits and research in the locations I write about. In some instances, names and minor details have been changed at the request of those involved. I use transliterations for a number of Arabic words in this book, and have chosen to not italicize these so that the reader can immerse themselves in the language and culture of the communities described in these pages, rather than being stopped at the difference of an italic word each time it is written. In several chapters, there are dialogue exchanges using transliterated Hindi, many of which are not translated. This is also intentional, as the text is written to support the reader in becoming immersed in the dialogue while providing ample context. I see the act of not italicizing non-English words as a way of acknowledging that words from many other languages are used in English. Also when writing about different linguistic communities, I prioritize expressing the experience of conducting the research, which in many instances has involved negotiating different languages.

The QR codes throughout the book will take you to the Soundcloud page for the field recordings associated with the page you are on. You should be able to scan the QR code with your smartphone camera or a QR code reader App. All of the field recordings are also available on the Soundmap of the Islamic Call to Prayer website at www.calltoprayersoundmap.com.

Short excerpts from this book have been published in an article in the *Journal of Sonic Studies* in 2019.[1]

(Image courtesy of Seersa Abaza).

Recording #0   Abu Darwish Mosque, Amman, Jordan. Book Cover Image.

Introduction

When I was twenty-three years old, I spent three months living and researching in India, during which time I became fascinated by religious recitations. For one month, I worked with fourth-grade English teachers at a girl's school and women's college in Rajasthan, and in my spare time, I conducted research on gender socialization in schooling environments for my master's thesis. One day after work, I climbed up to the rooftop of the college's guesthouse, and while looking out over the long main road and beyond toward the desert, I could hear the sounds of a celebration coming from a point just out of sight beyond the perimeter of the school. I later learned it was a Hindu wedding. As singing and drumming filled the air, I became lost in thought, hearing but not listening, such that the sounds in the distance became rhythms and sonic shapes beyond their words or notes. The longer I listened the more interested I became in the sounds of the wedding. I emerged from my thoughts with a recognition that I had heard those recitations before as a child. In that moment, the rhythmic recitation in what was likely Sanskrit or Hindi sounded identical to that of the cadence of the reading of the Hebrew Torah, which I had been so accustomed to, growing up Jewish and attending temple every Friday for Shabbat services. Later on, when I would become more familiar with the Islamic tartil readings from the Qur'an, I found similarities in sonic cadences and rhythms in those recitations as well. To me, all three seemed intuitively similar or at least linked. I present this moment of sonic epiphany as the precursor to the project that consumes the pages of this book.

Several years later, I packed my bags once again to move overseas, this time for a job in Abu Dhabi, the capital of the United Arab Emirates (UAE). The seed, an interest in the sounds of religion, had likely already been planted years before my realization that day on the rooftop in Rajasthan. I find that sometimes ideas or knowings, thoughts or feelings that we suspect must be important can lie dormant for some time. In my case, the idea of the connectedness and nuance of the sounds of religion had likely been a preoccupation for my mind for years, surfacing every so often as a flicker of knowing, and then quickly returning to its dormant state.

Shortly after my move to Abu Dhabi, I found myself completely enamored of the call to prayer, somewhat understandably, as it became a prominent element of my daily soundscape, impossible to miss, and at first very unfamiliar. I would routinely make the short walk from my skyscraper apartment building to the orange mosque just across the street, in order to listen to the sound of the adhan through the loudspeakers instead of muffled through the glass exterior of my apartment. On Fridays, the first day of the weekend in the Emirates, and the holiest day of the week in Islam, I would leave my apartment well in advance of the Jumu'ah Prayer that happened mid-day. Each Friday, I would wander through a different megablock to observe the prayer from a distance. I liked watching the men overflow the interior prayer room spaces of the mosque onto the entryway stairs and sometimes down into the streets. They were always in neat rows, shoulder to shoulder, wearing light-colored kandura standing or kneeling in front of individually laid prayer rungs. And I loved the moment when the adhan would sound and everything in the megablock seemed to pause. The cars weaving their way through the interior maze-like roads would stop, taxis would pull over, and people would take a break. I decided to send some of my audio recordings of the call to prayer to my family and friends back home, hoping it would give them a bit of context for my life and that they might also appreciate the adhan.

This was 2010, nine years after the 9/11 attacks on the World Trade Center in New York City. While I was living my daily life in the UAE, a Muslim country, enjoying the five times daily recitation of the adhan, I misjudged the way the sound of the call to prayer, out of context, might be heard. How it would be heard by New Yorkers less than a decade after 9/11, by people who themselves had no connection to Islam, and how it would be received by my Jewish family, who were living in a moment in time when their knowledge and understanding about Islam was most prominently shaped by the United States' "War on Terror," and by the constant and often biased reporting on the conflict between and occupation of Palestine by Israel.

I understood that it was probably impossible for my friends back in the United States to understand the feeling of becoming accustomed to hearing the adhan five times a day, and more than that, for it to become something I looked forward to, something that marked the day and something I found beautiful. I could explain how being in Abu Dhabi and hearing the morning Fajr adhan before my body was even awake affected me, but they could not feel those same effects. I realized the chasm between my experience, interest, and understanding of Islam and that of my family and friends grew larger the longer I was away. I also felt a tension inside myself, like an attraction of two opposing forces. This attraction was the tension between my identification as a Jew based in my upbringing, my growing interest in Islam spurred by living in countries with large Muslim communities, and a growing understanding of my own blood connection to Islam through my father's family, the last of which I grew up knowing nothing about yet somehow gravitated toward anyway.

My father was raised in Williamsburg, Brooklyn, where his family were members of the American Mohammedan Society, now known as the Moslem Mosque Inc., the oldest mosque in New York. My great-grandfather helped found the mosque in 1907, and my grandfather served as president of the mosque for a short time in the mid-1950s. My grandparents met and married in this community, and my father and uncle were raised going to prayers and masjid social events. The Moslem Mosque Inc. no longer sounds the adhan, due to an aging and dwindling membership, though just recently it began to livestream the recitation of the adhan and the prayers for major holidays.

The pages you are about to read provide an interior look inside a ten-year-long research project focused on making field recordings of the Islamic call to prayer at mosques around the world. The book is broken into chapters that are focused on geography and approaches to conducting the research. Within these chapters, the reader is given a glimpse into different Muslim communities through the author's lens. That lens, my lens, is that of an American who was raised in the Jewish faith and who still identifies as a Jew culturally, someone who is Queer and does not strongly identify within the gender binary, but often identifies as female in cultural contexts where the binary is a forgone conclusion. Someone who is white, and often passes as white, with mixed-race heritage, dark features, high cheek bones and almond shaped eyes, a sound scholar, an ethnographer, and an artist. My lens is informed by my upbringing as a New Yorker, a place of immigrants, an identification shared by my great-grandparents on both sides, and as a non-Muslim descendant of the Muslim Lipka Tatar community, some of whom, like my paternal great grandparents, emigrated to the United States from current-day Lithuania, Belarus, and Poland in the late nineteenth and early twentieth centuries (figure I.1 and recording 1).

The research that informs the writing of this book was conducted using ethnographic methods. Through these pages, you will read an intricately woven web of fieldwork, documentation, interviews, and conversations with people in the communities that I have visited. Unlike long-term ethnographic studies, during which I've spent months at a time in a place, many of the case studies in this book occurred in the span of several hours. Some are of short visits in communities where I have spent extended lengths of time, while others document an afternoon spent somewhere I had never previously been. There is an added layer of chronology in the book that is worth taking note

Figure I.1 Moslem Mosque Inc. (MMI) Brooklyn, New York, United States.

of. The dates of each case study place them in the arc of the overall project, as well as historically contextualize them based on world and local events. This arc includes events that have impacted Muslim communities and have contributed to the way Islam has been seen in a global context over the past twenty years, as well as events that have happened more privately. This arc simultaneously articulates creative and methodological process, the temporality of project, research, and process, and of course, my own personal growth as an artist and a researcher.

The reader is taken on a researcher's journey of first-encounter discovery and learns about the art of field recording in different contexts. The book is organized as a series of case studies of individual communities, intended

Recording #1 Moslem Mosque Inc. (MMI) Brooklyn, New York, United States.

to make the most sense in the context of the whole. My hope is that after completing this book, readers will have a deeper, more complex entry point into Islam, and into sound as a medium for research. Through these detailed personal accounts, I offer my approach as a method for conducting research, which has entangled and complex reaches into a variety of disciplines and creative practices. This approach foregrounds the value of bringing our whole selves to our research practice, the importance of ethical intention as a guide for the work, and the recognition that we will make mistakes and get things wrong.

Chapter 1

Recording Sound in Context
Soundmapping

To fear Muslims is not to fear someone thousands of miles away, but to not understand your neighbor.

The soundmap of the call to prayer is a web-based repository for all of the field recordings I made while conducting this research. The map lives online and is updated with new contributions. The initial idea for the map was very simple. Just like recordings of the adhan I sent to my family and friends back home, this online map was conceived of as a means of challenging Islamophobic assumptions. I had postulated that through sound, a medium I know to be extremely powerful and one that can impact people's emotions—think of dramatic sound effects that make us scared in horror movies—one could be challenged to rethink biases. While this may seem a bit idealistic, it was an initial kernel of an idea, and every good project needs one.

Whether or not the soundmap has succeeded in challenging Islamophobic assumptions, I can't say. However, it has grown beyond that initial kernel and is now a selection of representations of Muslim communities in different geographies, one that takes the call to prayer as its starting point. The soundmap offers sonic snapshots into a wide variety of countries, cultures, languages, topographies, and communities. Each recording is a documentation of place and the people in it, that when listened to carefully provides a wealth and depth of information, often beyond the walls of the prayer room or minaret from where the muezzin recited the adhan. The map as a whole is an evolving document and soundscape centered around mosques. Some of these mosques are ornate architectural centers of communities, and others are embedded in small storefronts, in villages, and on university campuses, each having a story. While this project is not focused on the architecture of mosques, many of the field recordings on the map reveal unique sonic resonances nodding to the spaces in which they were recorded. And the photographs included on the soundmap, some of which are presented in this book, highlight distinct Islamic styles of architecture that have traveled from their place of origin or have been brought into diasporic contexts.

The visual aspect of using a map of the world as a landing place for the field recordings was itself intentional. Maps reveal proximity, borders, expanse, and distance. They serve as a container in which to understand relationships between places. These relationships are not only between places highlighted on the map, but between those places and the ones we each individually have special connections to or call "home." The soundmap, ever-growing, does not intend to be a reference of all mosques in the world, nor does it successfully, at this point, represent every continent and country, though that is a goal. The map does, however, bring the visual and voice of certain mosques around the world to a broader audience in a frame that recognizes the geographic relationship of these mosques to one another, and to everywhere else in the world. The soundmap is easy to navigate and zoom in and out of, easy to locate oneself on and then look at other locations in relation. One intention of the map is to show, at a quick glance, that Islamic communities exist all over the world, perhaps in places one might not have thought (figure 1.1).

The call to prayer is part of our global soundscape. From New York City to a university campus in Ghana, to a rural village in India, it is a constant, live, sonic element that shapes the aural landscape of place. This project began in Abu Dhabi, where there is a mosque on practically every corner and the adhan sounds five times a day. In Abu Dhabi, I would travel around the city on bicycle and by car, capturing sounds from different corners of the city. Then I began to plan my international travel based around mosques I could visit to record the adhan. Initially it was just me traveling to Muslim communities, often alone, recording the adhan, taking photographs, and then returning home. The project expanded by necessity as it became clear that making all of the recordings alone would not allow for the project to expand and grow geographically in the ways I had hoped.

In 2013, I reached out to friends and colleagues from around the world, asking if they would contribute to the soundmap by recording the adhan and taking an accompanying photograph. People responded to the project with enthusiasm, but only a handful submitted recordings. I think this is in part due to the fact that the process of recording the adhan does require a certain level of patience and commitment, as I will speak about in the case studies later on in the book. Facebook became the primary platform for sharing the project, linking people to the soundmap, and requesting support to grow the collection of recordings. This approach had more reach than word of mouth, and touched many people well beyond my grasp, as friends re-posted and shared the project with their friends, with some even pointedly requesting others

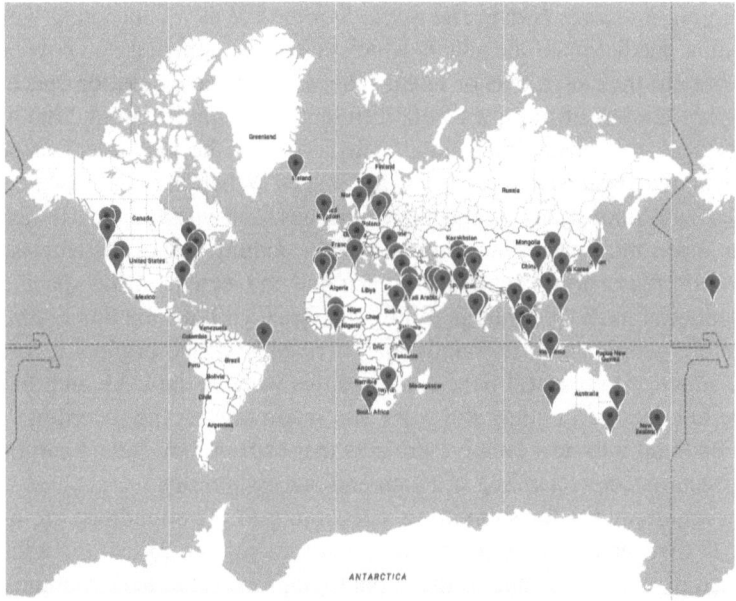

Figure 1.1 Soundmap of the Islamic Call to Prayer.

to submit recordings. Students of mine, after learning of the project, would contribute recordings and ask friends of theirs to do the same.

To date, the soundmap project includes recordings of the adhan from six continents and over forty countries, including New Zealand, Australia, Indonesia, Malaysia, Singapore, the Philippines, Cambodia, Myanmar, Hong Kong, China, Japan, India, Pakistan, Afghanistan, Oman, the United Arab Emirates, Qatar, Saudi Arabia, Israel, Jordan, Cyprus, Turkey, Italy, Belarus, Poland, Italy, Denmark, Ireland, Sweden, Iceland, Sudan, Tanzania, South Africa, Ghana, Tunisia, Morocco, Brazil, Canada, and the United States.

As the collection of field recordings of the call to prayer has grown, its reach has extended beyond the soundmap and into gallery spaces. The

Website Soundmap of the Islamic Call to Prayer.

exhibition, *Sounding Islam: The Sonic Storyboard*, is a conceptual work on the human mediation of the adhan, which offers a commentary on how people contribute to their own bias of Islam. The walls of the exhibition space hold large photographs of mosques from different communities around the world; below them are sensors that numerically quantify the movement of people as they walk toward or away from the images. When the space is empty, it is filled with unobstructed images of mosques, and one can clearly hear the adhan, often multiple adhan, the recordings coming out of different speakers around the space. People's presence and movement in the space cause augmentation to the recordings, filling the space with a sometimes subtle, or with more people an eerie soundscape, derived from the original recordings of the adhan. At present, I have exhibited this work in the UAE and Sweden. I hope to continue iterating the work and incorporating the recordings from the soundmap into new creative projects that explore how sound can impact and affect our understanding of Islam and our own biases.

The requirements for submitting a recording to the soundmap are as follows: 1) that the adhan be recorded live and in person, 2) that the adhan be recorded in its entirety, and 3) that a photograph be submitted from the place or position where the recording was made. As all recordings on the soundmap were made live and in context, the true grit and noise of the environment of each place is carefully captured in these recordings. These can include ambient street noise, sound system distortion, and the voices of others on the interior or exterior of those spaces delineated for prayer. The quality of the adhan, as heard by the recordist and captured by the recorder, is heavily influenced by the spaces inside of the mosque where the microphones are placed, and when used, the quality of the amplification system that carries the adhan through speakers outward to the community.

One of the grittiest adhan I have recorded, and also one of the most interesting, was from a mosque on the Jebel Akhdar mountain range in Oman. The recording captures the grit of the mountaintop village that appeared to house the only nearby inhabitants, the wall that surrounded their homes, and the craggy rock that surrounded that wall. It captures the way the sound from the speakers bounces off that wall, as the large modern mosque stands 20 meters away; it also captures the complete silence of the place, devoid of any human voices or movements other than that of the muezzin. To a listener, this adhan might not sound interesting, nor be the most beautiful. But when I listen to this adhan, I am transported back to that moment on the mountain, when after waiting for a long time I saw a man in a crinkly white kandura emerge from a cutout in the stone wall. He walked slowly, his head wrapped in a white keffiyeh. I imagined he did so to keep himself warm in the cold mountain air, and his teeth were stained red and brown likely from smoking shisha. He walked in a straight line from the wall to the mosque, and a few minutes after

Recording Sound in Context 5

Recording #2   Mosque Jebel Akhdar, Oman—Asr Adhan.

he entered the building, I heard the click of the amplification system turn on. What followed was the sound of his hurried raspy voice reciting the adhan, which was projected out of old wind-worn and sand-blasted speakers affixed to the outside of the mosque, riddled with cracks and pops (recording 2).

It is precisely because a listener would not have the same experience hearing the Jebel Akhdar recording as that of the recordist (in this case, me) that I decided to write a book that takes the reader and the listener through the cumulative journey of this research process. That journey began years before the research project was conducted and is deeply embedded in memories and experiences like the Hindu wedding overheard from the rooftop. In the chapters that follow, you will read about the ethnographic research process and learn more about my approach to documentation and recording. You will read backstories about how I ended up in certain geographic locations, and you will bear witness to gut checks as my research practice unfolds. The case studies I share in this book are all true accounts, each offering a different entry point into a Muslim community and each offering a different entry point into a scholarly creative process, including the learnings that informed how this research was done and how these recordings were made.

Chapter 2

Dahab, Egypt, 2003

I was twenty years old, and I had only ever left the United States twice before. The first time was on a week-long trip to Paris with my mother when I was eighteen—a high school graduation present. And the second was to Nicaragua during the winter break of my junior year of college to visit the host family of a friend who had taken time off to live there.

I grew up in an upper-middle-class, majority-white community for most of my childhood, and was surrounded by classmates who would regularly travel internationally with their families over school holidays. Many of my peers would talk about their family trips to the Caribbean, usually the Bahamas or Bermuda, while others traveled to resorts in Cancun, Mexico. Nicaragua was the road less traveled from the vantage point of my suburban town, and so when my college friend asked if I would like to travel there with her over the winter break, I said yes, of course yes. My mom was not too happy with my decision to travel to Nicaragua, but she was glad I was traveling with a friend who spoke Spanish better than I, and who knew the place well. We spent three weeks in Nicaragua, much of it in the Northwest city of Esteli, and a week on the la Isla de Ometepe, located in the middle of the Lago Cocibolca, a huge lake in the southeast of the country near the Costa Rican border.

It was in Nicaragua that I first learned how to wash clothes with a bar of soap on a big stone at an outdoor sink. It was also there that I first learned how the U.S. government backed the Contras and had a large hand in creating the circumstances that led to thousands of Sandinista Revolutionaries being killed. In Esteli, there was a Sandinista museum named "Asociación de ex-combatientes históricos 18 de Mayo." The small museum served as a memorial to many of the Esteli Sandinista Revolutionaries who died during the war. It was small but full of photographs and newspaper clippings of those who had died. My friend pointed out the photographs of her host mother's brother and other family members whose photographs hung in the museum. I remember feeling surprised and humbled by how the family, after all of the loss and destruction caused by the U.S.-backed Contra groups, welcomed us young Americans into their home with open arms. My friend's host mother explained how she saw our government's actions as distinctly separate from those of the people of our country. This is a sentiment I would hear many times again over the following years.

A year later, I applied to Taglit, Birthright Israel, in the hopes of being granted an all-expenses-paid ten-day trip to Israel. The program's stated aim is to bring young Jewish people to Israel to strengthen Jewish Identity, and while on the trip, I heard others talking about the possibility of making aliyah, moving to Israel to live. The Birthright group was made up of fifteen students and three group leaders. We all flew into Ben Gurion Airport and took a chartered bus to our hotel in Jerusalem, where we spent the first half of our ten-day trip. The Birthright group I was assigned to was arguably one of the most secular, if one could make that argument.

The first few days of the trip were full of visits to historical sites, food, and listening to our guide talk about the geography of the country. In the evenings, the group leaders orchestrated approved activities that, while left of center, felt Zionistic in their nature. I remember one evening activity in particular. The leaders of our group placed a huge paper map on the carpet of the meeting room at the hotel. We talked about The Green Line, where it was drawn, the politics of it, and what it meant. I remember trying desperately to piece things together in my head, to determine if what we were being told was an unbiased truth, or a blatantly biased perspective. I recall leaving that evening's conversation and several others, not only feeling uneasy to be learning such information about conflict and occupation through games, but also not knowing how to contextualize what we were being told, given the purpose and aim of this free trip to Israel.

There were six of us who decided not to board the plane back to the United States, but to instead travel to Egypt through a border crossing at Taba, which was a bus ride from the southern city of Eilat. When we reached the border crossing, we had to proceed on foot through an interior passageway that had Israeli military posted at the front end, and Egyptian military on the back end. We had to place our bags on scanners to leave Israel, and we ourselves were scanned. We were asked a few questions and were permitted to pass into Egypt, which was the act of walking a few feet forward. We had been told explicitly to ask the Egyptian border patrol not to place a stamp in our passports as this would make traveling back into Israel easier when we left to catch our flights home.

The Egyptian border patrol was a different experience entirely. The Egyptian military was much more scrutinizing of our bags and belongings. They went through every item in my bag right down to flipping through pages in my personal journal. When we emerged from the immigration crossing, there was a line of old beat-up minivans waiting on the dirt road. We had decided we would travel to Dahab, a larger seaside town on the Sinai Peninsula where we could relax and dip our feet into the Gulf of Aqaba. We had heard Dahab was beautiful with a well-appointed town, an abundance of restaurants and small shops, and proximity to beautiful coral reefs that were good for snorkeling. The six of us piled into a van driven by a Druid who the Israeli soldier friend traveling with us thought was trustworthy. The driver piled our suitcases on top of the van, tying them down with rope, and we took off down the Dahab Nuweiba Road. The driver, without any discussion, took us to a small lodge in Nuweiba that was by the water and still being constructed. We piled out of the van, relieved to have a break from the hot bumpy ride. We eagerly explored the water and had cooling drinks. Then we piled back into the van and continued down the road.

Finally, we arrived in Dahab. The minivan dropped us near a restaurant, on the beach. Our first priority was to find a place to sleep for that first night. One of the other women and I decided to stay in these straw huts, one block inland from the beach, which ran us $5.00 per night. They were clean, felt safe, and were within our price range. Everyone decided to stay in different places. The plan was that we would all meet back at the restaurant where the van had dropped us so that we could have a proper meal. The Dahab beach was beautiful, and the restaurants were all right on the beach. Upholstered furniture was placed directly on the sand oriented like it would be in a living room, with a long couch facing the ocean, armchairs placed at either side facing toward one another, and a coffee table in between. The cooks had a metal drum barbeque set up on the sand where they grilled fish and meat, the smell of which mixed with the warm salty air. The trip was off to a wonderful start and my initial uneasiness about visiting Egypt had subsided.

Our first night's sleep was relatively uneventful and on the second day, we went snorkeling at the Blue Hole. Four of us piled into the jeep, which took us on a beautiful rocky mountain drive to a large expanse of stunning blue ocean. The jeep drove us right up to the only thing at the Blue Hole, a dive shop, or maybe it was two dive shops side by side that rented out scuba and snorkeling gear, and where we could get french fries and a drink. We rented snorkeling masks and stripped down to our bathing suits. I remember cutting myself on the coral on the way into the water and worrying that it might be that killer coral I had heard about that would start eating away at my flesh. It wasn't, and I was fine.

On our last day in Dahab, we decided to explore on foot, beyond the beach and the main market street. We walked inland several blocks to see what else there was beyond the touristy main strip. As it turned out, there wasn't much at all. The buildings became shorter and fewer as we walked inland, and after the third block, we found nothing except mountains surrounding us and flat land in front of us. We stumbled onto the front porch of what I thought at the time looked like an old closed concrete post office. We were all in need of shade from the hot midday sun, and the overhang on the front porch of the building was the perfect respite. We sat there for a while chatting, discussing the town of Dahab and our adventures.

There was a sudden loud screeching noise; it was someone screaming over a loudspeaker. I found myself back in that panicky heart racing space I was in at the border crossing. I dropped to the ground, or at least I think I did. I can't remember those moments clearly. The loud screeches continued. I looked around; I was sure that someone had discovered us, the Jews from the United States and the Israeli soldier. The narrative in my head was that we had ventured too far from the safety of the tourist-oriented main town and were in a less safe area where we were not welcome. I was waiting for the sound of gunshots to ring out. The screaming voice once again came over the loudspeaker and I saw the others begin to run back toward the beach. I got to my feet, heart pounding in my gut, and ran after them. My legs felt like molasses, as though I was in one of those fear dreams where I was so scared that I couldn't seem to run or get away from the people chasing me. As we made our way the three or four blocks back toward the beach, we stopped running and caught our breath. No one said a word. We walked slowly now, back to the beach restaurant and sat down for a final meal before our departure. One person ordered a Shisha pipe, and we all got beers.

It took me a few minutes to realize that what I was hearing was not directed at us at all. It took me a few years more to realize that what I had heard that day was most likely the adhan. It wasn't until 2009, when I was bicycling around Abu Dhabi recording the adhan, that the disturbance and distortion of the recitation through the loudspeaker systems of a local mosque triggered my memory of that experience in Sinai, and helped me realize that, most likely, what I heard that day was the call to prayer.

Chapter 3

Mosque Alarm Clock

Abu Dhabi, United Arab Emirates, 2011

One Saturday afternoon roughly a year after moving to Abu Dhabi, I embarked on a search for an adhan alarm clock. I was intrigued by the concept of an alarm clock that was intended to be set to remind one of the prayer time. I traveled to a small inner megablock shop, the kind that was closed for the afternoon break between 1 pm and 4 pm, and which was stocked from floor to ceiling with different types of clocks. The shop was on a small side street near the Madinat Zayed Gold Souq and across from a Qur'anic bookshop, where one could purchase Qur'an, prayer rugs, and prayer beads.

The clock shop was tiny and rectangular. I had to step up into the shop off the sidewalk out front, into the rectangular area on the customer's side of the counter. This space was so narrow that when another person entered the shop, it became necessary for the two customers to dance around one another in order to pass, like in the aisle of an airplane. Across the counter was the shopkeeper on his side of the shop, where he was surrounded in a semicircle of kitsch mismatching clocks and watches of all sizes, shapes, and colors. The clocks were arranged on the long wall behind the shop owner and on the two short sidewalls on either side. The special items, often of greater value, were prominently displayed inside the glass-topped counter so that customers would see them when they entered.

I walked in and nodded hello, as the shopkeeper was helping another customer. I quickly redirected my gaze away from the shopkeeper and up toward the clocks. I did a quick visual scan of everything that was there, much of it easy to glance over. There were many round wall clocks and ugly metal-framed contemporary clocks with numbers in strange fonts. I could hear the shopkeeper speaking to the customer in Hindi, a very common occurrence in Abu Dhabi. While the customer was investigating several different options, the shopkeeper asked me what I was looking for, and I told him an adhan alarm clock. He grabbed a small white box off of the shelf and carefully opened it to reveal a square gray table-top alarm clock, smaller than a deck of playing cards, and with a flip-out stand. The alarm clock allowed you to pick a geography, and it then sounded the adhan at the appropriate prayer time. The functionality of the alarm clock matched what I wanted, but the clock was not aesthetically interesting, and the sound of the recorded adhan was mechanical, sounding like a cross between an 8-bit video game and a scratched vinyl record.

Between the almost floor-to-ceiling cabinets along the back wall and the ceiling, there was a layer of clocks that were displayed inches from the overhead lights. There I saw it, the mosque alarm clock I had imagined in my mind. It was green plastic in the shape of a mosque, with two minarets. In the center of the mosque was a clock face, and above it a large golden dome.

> "Jee, yeh wala dekhana," I pointed up to the mosque-shaped alarm clock asking to see it.

He pointed to a silver oval clock on the wall, and I pointed upward.

> "Yeh hara wala," I said.

He climbed on the countertop and reached toward something on top of the shelves, looking down at me to see if it was the right one.

> "Right side, right side," I said. He put his hand on the box to the right and looked down at me for approval. "Haanji."

He brought down a box from behind the clock and placed it on the countertop in front of me. He unpacked the box and pulled out a shiny baby pink mosque alarm clock, smaller than the one on display. I studied the pink plastic mosque, with its gold-colored trim, and the thatched texture that was built into the mold indicating a border around the mosque. The tiny minarets jutted up from the left and right of the clock, and in the center, there was a small round golden dome.

> "Doosra hai?" [Is there another?], I asked. "Hara rung chahiye" [I want a green colored one], I continued.

The shopkeeper searched above and found a larger dark green mosque alarm clock more similar to the one on display. He placed the box on the glass countertop and pulled the mosque out of the box. It was regal and perfect. I turned the clock around, switched on the alarm setting, and then turned the

Figure 3.1 Mosque Alarm Clock, United Arab Emirates.

alarm clock hand to two minutes ahead of the current time. We waited. The adhan sounded. It was loud, clear, and perfect (figure 3.1 and recording 3).

The shopkeeper was most likely a migrant worker in Abu Dhabi from South Asia, who spent his days behind that desk selling clocks. He certainly wasn't in it for citizenship or to retire in the Emirates. Immigration possibilities like that weren't available to foreigners in the UAE. And the story of our interaction, while seemingly benign, paints a picture—a backdrop of Abu Dhabi, the place, its small streets, with clock shops and Islamic stores behind Gold Souqs. A place where Hindi is spoken with greater frequency than Arabic, and where the sleek digital is prized and thought to be more in demand than the old and analog. These details, seemingly small, weave their way through

Recording #3 Mosque Alarm Clock, Abu Dhabi, United Arab Emirates.

the pages of this book, in an attempt to paint a story of each place, to give insight into the content of the place beyond the mosque that is visited, and beyond the details of Islam or the way it is practiced. These details are a key element of the methodology of the writing of this book, along with the use of translation and descriptions of linguistic interactions that occur in the process of making field recordings of the adhan.

Chapter 4

Sounding the Adhan

One of the intentions for creating the soundmap of the call to prayer was to capture the nuance of the adhan in different places in the world. I attempt to do this by highlighting the beauty of the recitation and the diversity of the outward-facing sounds of Islam, the thing that for many non-Muslims may be their only connection to the religion. Adhan, the Islamic call to prayer, is recited five times daily as a way of signifying to Muslims that it is time to pray. Salah, prayer, is one of the five pillars of Islam, to be performed five times daily while facing the direction of Mecca. Salah can be done anywhere, either privately or in the company of others, and depending on the individual interpretation, the prayer times can signify when one should pray, or the time between each call can serve as a window in which one should pray. The five daily prayers span from before the sun rises to after the sun sets, and are dictated by the sun, making the timings different daily and in every geography. The prayer times are known as Fajr, the early morning prayer (before sunrise); Dhuhr, the noontime prayer; Asr, the late-afternoon prayer; Maghreb, the sunset prayer; and Isha'a, the late-evening prayer.

> In almost every Islamic community today the loudspeaker, radio and television have become essential in the traditional call to prayer, a remarkable juxtaposition of high media technology and conservative religious practice. The loudspeaker simply extended the purpose of the minaret, that towering section of the mosque where the reciter traditionally stood to perform the call to prayer, his voice reaching the surrounding Islamic community.
>
> —Toong Soon Lee (1999)[1]

Historically the call to prayer served as a "soundmark,"[2] which sonically defined the boundary of a given Islamic community, based on the area over which the muezzin's voice could be heard. Whereas traditionally the muezzin, or reciter of the call to prayer, recited the adhan from the top of the mosque's minaret, in modern day, many muezzin recite the adhan into a microphone which is then broadcast over loudspeakers, affixed to the mosque's façade or the top of a minaret, facing outward toward the community. There are many mosques in which the adhan is not recited out toward the community, but rather inside the prayer room in the direction of Mecca. In contemporary urban contexts, where people may not live or work within earshot of a mosque, technological aides are used to keep track of prayer times, including Islamic radio stations, adhan alarm clocks, and smartphone apps that contain the call to prayer times for geographies around the world.

In his book *Approaching the Qur'an: The Early Revelation*, Michael Sells discusses the importance of the recitation of the adhan as "one of the most venerated activities within Islamic culture and civilization."[3] There are specific rules of recitation that guide the reading of the Qur'an. After speaking with several Imams and pious Muslims, my understanding is that the way the adhan is recited is not specified in the Qur'an, but rather it is mentioned in the Hadith that the adhan should be recited beautifully. Some Muslims I have asked say that this has been interpreted to mean it should be recited by the man in the community with the most beautiful voice.

Figure 4.1 Tightmarte Village, Morocco.

Recording #4 Tightmarte Village, Morocco, Example of Tartīl Style of Recitation.

Though the recitation style of the adhan varies by country and individual muezzin, as is evident through the diverse recordings on the soundmap, there are two broad categories of recitation that I have noticed through my research. These seem to be related to the Qur'anic recitation styles of the tartīl and the tajwīd. The tartīl is an extremely powerful style, characterized by a steady chant, while the tajwīd, or tajawwud, is a highly elaborate style boasting elaborate vocal extensions and flourishings.[4] It is fairly easy to sonically identify these overarching stylistic differences in recitations, as the tartīl style recitations tend to be faster and therefore shorter, whereas the tajwīd style recitations tend to be more elongated with flourishings and in this way, they carry a familiar sonic quality that is easily identifiable when recited. It is also worth mentioning that while the adhan is a call to prayer, each time the adhan is recited it is followed roughly fifteen minutes later by the iqamah, the final call to prayer, which is often spoken quickly to indicate that the prayer will now begin. The iqamah has a different phrasing to the adhan, one that is shorter and more pointed toward the immediacy of the start of the prayer. You can listen to examples of these two different styles of recitation in recordings 4 and 5 (figures 4.1 and 4.2 and recordings 4 and 5).

The adhan is a call out to the community that it is time to make salah. The words of the adhan, which are broken into phrases, have the clear purpose of venerating God and reminding people to pray. I am familiar with two versions of the adhan, one for Sunnis and one for Shiites, though I am most familiar with the Sunni adhan as it is the one that has sounded in the majority of mosques I have visited. The Sunni adhan has twelve phrases, while the Shiite adhan has sixteen phrases. Each muezzin, regardless of where they are located in the world or their recitation style, will recite the same adhan phrases, either using the Sunni or Shiite versions. The one exception to all of this is a phrase that is added only to the Fajr (early morning) Adhan, which sounds roughly an hour and twenty minutes before sunrise. The phrase, Assalatu Khairum Minan Naum [Prayer is better than sleep] is recited twice before the final two phrases of the adhan. This line is only recited for the early morning prayer as an encouragement to get out of bed and pray.

Figure 4.2 Akuafo Hall Mosque, University of Ghana Legon, Accra, Ghana.

The difference between the Shiite adhan and Sunni adhan is two phrases, each recited twice. Both versions begin and end exactly the same with the first phrase, Allahu Akbar, Allahu Akbar [God is most great, God is most great], which is recited twice. This is followed by Ashadu an la ilaha illa Allah [I witness that there is no God but God (Allah)], recited twice, and then Ashadu anna Muhammadan Rasool Allah [I witness that Muhammad is the messenger of God], recited twice. After this sixth phrase, the two versions of the adhan start to differ. Namely, the Shiite version of the adhan has four additional phrases not found in the Sunni adhan. The first additional phrase which follows the initial six verses is Ash-Hado Annal Aliyan Wali-Y'Allah

Recording #5 Akuafo Hall Mosque, University of Ghana Legon, Accra, Ghana, Example of Tajwīd Style of Recitation.

[I bear witness that Ali is representative of Allah], which is repeated twice. This is followed by four phrases that are the same in both adhan, Hayya A'lassalaah [Come to prayer], repeated twice, and Hayya A'lalfallah [Come to prosperity] repeated twice. In the Shiite adhan, the next phrase, also repeated twice, is Hayya A'la Khayril Amal [Hasten toward the best of action]. Both adhan conclude with the following two verses: Allahu Akbar, Allahu Akbar [God is most great, God is most great], La ilaha illa Allah [There is no God but God].

THE ADHAN الأذان (SUNNI VERSION)

God is most Great, God is most Great	الله أكبر، الله أكبر
God is most Great, God is most Great	الله أكبر، الله أكبر
I witness that there is no God but God (Allah)	أشهد أن لا إله إلا الله
I witness that there is no God but God (Allah)	أشهد أن لا إله إلا الله
I witness that Muhammad is the messenger of God	أشهد أن محمدًا رسولُ الله
I witness that Muhammad is the messenger of God	أشهد أن محمدًا رسولُ الله
Come to prayer	حيَّ على الصلاة
Come to prayer	حيَّ على الصلاة
Come to Prosperity	حيَّ على الفلاح
Come to Prosperity	حيَّ على الفلاح
God is most Great, God is most Great	الله أكبر، الله أكبر
There is no God but God[5]	لا إله إلا الله

The recordings of the adhan you will hear in this book capture sounds beyond the parameters of the call to prayer. These recordings are a documentation of a particular place in a moment in time, and I might go as far as to say they are a recorded soundscape. This is a critical distinction that will allow me to discuss the sonic qualities and relevance of these recordings using language that speaks about the recordings as types of compositions, without referring to the adhan itself as musical. From an ethical perspective, this is important as the call to prayer is considered a religious recitation and not musical in Islam. Therefore, when I refer to the recordings of the adhan in this book, I am speaking of something altogether different from the adhan, the recitation of the call to prayer. I am speaking about a translation of this recitation, which I have made by way of capturing an audio recording in a place in a particular moment in time. That recording is itself a completely new thing, not a religious recitation but rather a recording of a religious recitation in a particular community. It is these elements of place and community that I will focus on in the following chapters.

Chapter 5

Old Fish Market, Abu Dhabi, United Arab Emirates, 2010

W2 Mosque, in the Old Fish Market of Abu Dhabi, was a small blue-tiled mosque next to a fruit stand and behind Panda Panda, a favorite Chinese food lunch spot. I passed W2 Mosque on my bike every day and had no idea what it was called, nor can I recall ever seeing anyone go in or out. Google Maps does not have street view access in the UAE; however, it does have accurate maps and landmarks, which is where I found the name W2, and more recently in tiny Arabic scrawl in the metadata, the name Masjid Thabit bin Amr. I have learned that mosques in Abu Dhabi are named after people, often members of the royal family, and sometimes places. For example, the large and very grand mosque situated diagonally across the megablock from W2 is the Sheikh Khalifa Mosque. Sheikh Khalifa bin Zayed Al Nahyan is the president of the UAE and the son of the founder of the UAE, Sheikh Zayed bin Sultan Al Nahyan. I have been told that before the Sheikh Zayed Grand Mosque was opened in 2007, the Sheikh Khalifa Mosque was the prominent mosque in the city.

    The Sheikh Khalifa Mosque is across the parking lot from the front entrance of what at that time was the New York University Abu Dhabi Downtown Campus, or the DTC for short. Most days, while eating lunch outside in the courtyard of the DTC where I worked, I would hear the adhan sound from the mosque. It was loud, imposing, and took up sonic space. Because there are so many mosques in Abu Dhabi, often more than one per megablock, it isn't rare to hear a multitude of adhan sounding on top of one another, as was the case from the DTC outdoor lunch tables. I could hear at least two, maybe three, adhan sounding simultaneously in very close proximity and could usually hear another one or two faintly in the distance, their soundwaves seemingly carried by the wind from blocks away. The cacophony of sound swelled, the frequencies of the call taking up all of the vibrating space in the air. Our lunch table chatting would fall quiet during the adhan, not because of the religious nature of the moment but because of the omnipresence of the sounds and the reality that to speak above the call to prayer would require yelling across the table. The sounding of the adhan does not ask for quiet, but rather it is meant to be loud as a signal to the community that the prayer time will soon begin (figure 5.1 and recording 6).

There are three mosques in the Old Fish Market megablock, the Sheikh Khalifa Mosque on the Khalid Bin Al Waleed Street side of the megablock, the Sheikh Hamed Bin Butti Mosque on the Airport Road side of the megablock, and the W2 Mosque behind the row of shops on the Khalifa Bin Zayed the First Street side of the megablock.

I rode my matte black single fork Cannondale bicycle to work every day. I had decided before I moved to the UAE that since I would be living near to where I worked, I wanted to commute on bike. I failed, however, to take into account the summer heat and how bicycle un-friendly the drivers in Abu Dhabi would be. I lived in the Madinat Zayed megablock in Sama Tower, or in English, Sky Tower, named for its towering height of forty-four stories, which made it the tallest building in Abu Dhabi when it was built. The campus was two large megablocks away from Sama Tower, toward the corniche. Airport Road is one of the busiest thoroughfares in Abu Dhabi City, snaking its way from the airport forty-five minutes outside of the city, all the way to

Figure 5.1 Sheikh Khalifa Mosque, Abu Dhabi, United Arab Emirates.

Old Fish Market, Abu Dhabi, United Arab Emirates, 2010 23

Recording #6   Sheikh Khalifa Mosque, Abu Dhabi, United Arab Emirates.

the beach on the Corniche Road at the center of the downtown. I was a little terrified to ride my bike in the bustling traffic but was committed to doing the five-minute commute by bicycle, rather than the twenty-minute walk in the heat.

My friend Michael and I started a tradition of early morning bicycle rides up and down the corniche promenade, the beautiful walkway that goes along the beach and waterfront from one end of Abu Dhabi city's downtown to the other. There is a bike lane on the corniche with a nice smooth surface, where we would fly up and down every morning. Our routine was to leave Sama Tower by 7 am, especially as the seasons started to change, and to ride down Airport Road going with traffic, until we hit the park in the middle of Airport Road down near the corniche. The park split the two-way traffic on the major roadway and housed two mosques, a parking lot, a nice green area with benches and fountains, and access to a pedestrian and bicycle underpass to the Corniche Road. My favorite part of the morning was riding through the park on weekends when the space was transformed into a cricket pitch by teams of South Asian men who would run between make-shift wickets in their beautiful white kurta pajamas, as the cloudless blue sky caught the minarets of the mosque behind them.

Once we crossed under the six-lane Corniche Road, we would alternate between going left toward the Marina Mall or right toward the Fish Market. The Marina Mall direction meant we would bicycle down to the end of the promenade and turn a hard right onto a side promenade, which we would follow around until it spit us out onto the street toward the National Theater. The theater was an old concrete dome building that sat at the edge of a parking lot which served as the starting point for a concrete pier. The pier jutted out into the Gulf, and on the right, there was a small sand beach where children would play on the weekends. Michael and I would walk down the pier to take in the panoramic morning views of the downtown of Abu Dhabi City. There was rarely anyone around, and our time was often spent in silence appreciating the views, the breeze, and hearing the waves crash up against the rough rocks. The streetlamps lining the pier dated back to the 1990s. Many of their glass globes were broken, adding to the aesthetic of the place, which had an element of the tangible and gritty. The pier and the National Theater were holdovers of an old Abu Dhabi, increasingly difficult to uncover amid the skyscrapers and shopping malls of the modern city. Stray cats and crabs were the primary morning inhabitants moving around and through the giant rocks, and after twenty minutes or so, we would jump back on our bikes and peddle back to Sama Tower in order to shower and change in time for work.

Heading right at the corniche, toward the fish market, was a slightly longer ride down the promenade with the glinting water of the Arabian Gulf on our left-hand side. At moments, the promenade had ramp ways down to areas closer to the water, and at others, we were pushed over bridges and onto narrower walkways toward the road. The promenade dead-ended into a small circle. We would often jump the curb and continue riding on the narrow sidewalk along the main street, eventually joining the street traffic as we headed toward the Fish Market. The Al Mina Fish Market, not to be confused with the Old Fish Market near W2 Mosque named after a now-demolished fish market, is a large indoor market with many vendors selling different kinds of raw fish and seafood. The area was usually bustling even at seven in the morning as everyone headed in to get fresh fish for the day. We would hang a left just past the fish market building, and cycle through the metal gates and off to the left where we rode along the backside of the boat and diving shops.

The fish market port was differently beautiful from the National Theater Pier. Here, there were wooden dhows lining the port, most with men living on them as was indicated by the lines of drying laundry. The men were hanging out waiting a few days before they would go back out on the water. Depending on the day, we would also usually find hundreds of chickenwire fishing traps being built and stored right on the road next to where the dhows docked. To ready the boats for their next trip, the traps would be loaded onto the boats, strung together and hung from the wooden frame. A new batch of fishermen would come back from several days out at sea, and the process would begin again. Michael and I would find a spot to sit and take in the ambiance. Occasionally, we would ride around the back, making our way past every shop and the worker accommodations, which sat two blocks back from the water.

I developed some reasonably safe techniques during those morning rides when the roads were less busy that I would later apply to my morning bike commute to work. Friday mornings and National Holidays are just about the only times when the streets of Abu Dhabi City are empty. Before the Jumu'ah Prayer on Fridays, one can basically use the city streets as their own personal triathlon training ground, and I knew a few people who did just that. I, on the other hand, used it as an opportunity to see the city by bike, which is otherwise a completely awful and unsafe idea. The first time I ventured out was on the Prophet Mohammed's birthday as the streets were empty and riding was a joy. I traveled all over the city, from the corniche end of the island toward the hinterlands, where megablocks of villas replaced glass-plated high-rise buildings and malls. I was so excited by the freedom of the ride that I decided I would take my bike out the following Friday morning with a recording rig to try and record an adhan from a mosque in the city.

I excitedly planned out my next bicycle outing. I borrowed a blue gear bag from the university and placed my Sound Devices 702T audio recorder, a stereo capsule microphone, a shock mount handle, a windscreen, cables, and some batteries into the bag, and slung it over my back. I set out on my bike that Friday morning, a little wobbly as I worked on balancing the weight of the gear, and I cycled through the streets. I was likely a site to behold, being on a black street bike, wearing a matching matte black skater helmet, most likely in jeans and a t-shirt with a big bag over my back. Not a typical Abu Dhabi street sighting.

I rode around the city for a while, with that whimsical feeling of there being nowhere I had to go, but also that strange, tethered feeling of being drawn to the places and things one already knows. After a twenty-minute ride around the downtown, I unsurprisingly ended up taking my daily bike commute path to the DTC. As I rounded the corner of Hamdan Street into the megablock, I pulled to the side of the road under the shade of the building and paused to take a drink of water and wipe the sweat from my face. I looked at my watch and realized the adhan was supposed to sound in ten minutes. I peddled over to the side of the DTC, across from W2, in the shade of the backup power generator building. I got off the bike and put down the gear bag in order to balance the kickstand-less bike against the wall. I sat on the curb and unpacked the items from the bag. I turned the recorder on, plugged the microphone and headphones into it, and powered everything on, before placing the recorder back in the bag. I swung the bag over my shoulder and stood up, angling the microphone toward the mosque.

Trying not to breathe too loudly, or to have to scratch an itch at the exact wrong moment, I waited. I am a stickler for getting a really high-quality, complete field recording, which captures the adhan in its entirety. Then I heard the call from behind me. It was the adhan from the Sheikh Khalifa Mosque diagonally across the megablock. I couldn't see the mosque but the adhan was loud and clear. There was still no adhan from W2 Mosque. I started to wonder if perhaps this little mosque was inactive, if maybe it never actually did sound, which would explain why I never saw anyone going in or out of it.

I sat back down on the curb frustrated that I had wasted my first recording morning on a defunct mosque with no adhan. I felt stupid for not stopping across the megablock at the Sheikh Khalifa Mosque. I got that feeling of regret inside and was thinking up another plan, knowing that the next adhan

Figure 5.2   W2 Mosque, Old Fish Market Megablock, Abu Dhabi, United Arab Emirates. *Source:* Image courtesy of Renji Jacob.

would not be for several hours and I would likely melt outside in the heat before that happened. Then, like a loud bus coming to a screeching halt, something came out of the speakers attached to the mosque right in front of me. I froze for a moment then instinctively readjusted the microphone in my hand so that it was pointing directly toward the mosque. I had slacked off in my moment of regret. I tried to control my breathing and become very still in my body so as to not record any noises of myself moving, fabric swishing, or handling noises of my grip on the microphone. The sound was overwhelmingly loud, or perhaps I was just too close to the mosque. Once I got the recording equipment properly adjusted, I stopped worrying and started listening. I only relaxed my posture after hearing the final click of the microphone switch being moved to the off position (figure 5.2 and recording 7).

Recording #7   W2 Mosque, Abu Dhabi, United Arab Emirates.

Old Fish Market, Abu Dhabi, United Arab Emirates, 2010

I was sitting on the stoop, in the shade, behind the DTC on a Friday morning with no one else in sight, recording the adhan from the small mosque with the blue-tiled dome. I smiled. No more regret washed over me; instead I felt elated. My bicycle recording adventure had been successful, and I felt empowered to continue on. I did continue on for many months and years after that initial adventure, riding my bicycle and carrying the recording gear around the city and around the world to record the call to prayer.

The W2 Mosque, like many things in Abu Dhabi City, has been renovated since I first recorded there in 2010. Figure 5.2 is what the mosque currently looks like. It is in the same location but has been updated significantly.

Chapter 6

Reykjavik, Iceland, 2017

I traveled to Iceland in 2016 and rented a van with a bed in the back, so that my girlfriend and I could drive around the Ring Road, the paved loop that circles the perimeter of the country. We had five days with the van, and made it from the airport to Reykjavik, on to the West of the country, then the North, and almost all the way to the East before having to turn around.

Iceland has the most stunning expanses, beautiful mountain passes, open fields of green and brown, hot sulfur pools in the most hidden and amazing locations, and splendid beauty unobstructed by humans for as far as the eye can see. One night we pulled the van off the road to the edge of what we could best make out to be a field. It was early morning maybe 2 am, but because of the long summer days, the sun had only just set.

Iceland is breathtaking, and there is something wonderful about the crisp Icelandic air after flying in from the rising summer temperatures in the Emirates. I knew I wanted to come back to Iceland and luckily had an opportunity to return the following summer with two phenomenal colleagues, as our panel "Found in Translation: Connecting Cultural Heritage and Community through Sight and Sound" was accepted to the 2017 NonFictionNow Conference held at the University of Iceland in Reykjavik.

On the first day of the conference, the opening remarks were given along with a toast in the main lobby of the Library building. Across the room, I spotted the conference organizer's wife Guðrún, whom I had met the year before. She had wonderfully styled blond hair, an artist's cut, and a funky yet outdoorsy style of dress. To avoid the awkward dance of not having any conversation to join, I walked toward the table where she was standing. She was lovely as I remembered her being, and we chatted about what we had been up to since we saw one another last. We caught up on life as we sipped our wines. She is an artist, and we moved seamlessly from discussions about the conference organizing she and her husband had been busy with in the months and weeks leading up to the conference, to a conversation about art in Iceland. She spoke about some of the work she had been doing with birds and some of the recent exhibitions she had visited. I mentioned my ongoing work with the soundmap to her, not remembering if I had mentioned it the year before. I asked if she was familiar with the mosques in Reykjavik. She said she thought there was one but didn't know anything about it. I told her that I had tracked down the location of a mosque and asked if she would be interested in going there with me and my friend Heidi. Guðrún, having never been to a mosque herself, was curious to see this mosque in her own city, and offered to drive us there the following day in her car. This was fantastic as taxis are expensive in Reykjavik, but also this meant that we would more likely make it on time.

I learned that there were two mosques in Reykjavik, and upon further investigation and research on Google Maps satellite view, I was able to find one of the two. In a country like Iceland with such a small Muslim population, it wouldn't be strange for the mosque to serve primarily as a gathering point for Jumu'ah prayer on Fridays, not necessarily for daily prayers.

The Dhuhr prayer was scheduled for 1:26 pm on June 1st, and it was only days before Ramadan. I always get nervous when I head out to record the adhan, because I worry I will run out of time. Traveling somewhere new can always take more time than anticipated and I like having ample time to meet the community members and set up my gear. Setting up the recording equipment takes time and cannot be rushed, as I like to check the recorder settings, battery life, storage capacity, recording format, and test the microphone levels before I begin. Depending on the recording gear I bring with me and the recording circumstances, this task of checking the equipment can be easier or more arduous a task.

At around 1:15 pm, we arrived at the address I had found for the mosque. There was a series of multilevel white buildings that all looked alike, so it took some time to figure out which building we were looking for. The mosque was in a commercial area, and all of the buildings had small placards near the front door with the names of the companies that had offices inside. I had learned at this point that in countries where Islam is a minority religion, mosques don't always have the architectural detail that make it outwardly obviously a mosque. In these situations, there are a few key things I look for. The first is speakers mounted externally on the building. Even if there are no clear signs or symbols on the outside to indicate that a building is a mosque, it may have an amplification system to sound the call to prayer into the community. The second is the color green, as green is often representative of Islam. I have noticed that mosques that exist in nontraditional structures either temporarily or permanently, often have the color green surrounding the entryway. This building had no external speakers, no green on the door, or any other signs that I could spot. Then I noticed it, a small white placard under a more formal logo of another company that read, Félag Múslima Á Íslandi.

The three of us walked into the building and up one flight of stairs, where I noticed several shoe racks outside the door. "This is probably the place," I said to Guðrún and Heidi. We were three women without headscarves, walking to the front door of a mosque in a commercial building in Reykjavik. I imagine we stuck out. I took my shoes off, placed them in the shoe rack in the hallway, and walked inside, leaving my travel companions in the hall for the moment. I could see the prayer room off to the left, and in front of me was an office. I made it three steps toward the office before a man walked toward me. I said hello and asked if the muezzin was there. The man didn't speak English very well and told me to wait. He brought out the Imam.

"Hello, I am Imam Ismaeel. I am the visiting Imam."

"Hi" I replied. "My name is Diana, I am here visiting with my two friends." I gestured toward the hallway. "We are hoping we can enter the mosque to record the adhan."

Ismaeel, as it turned out, was studying at a school in Mecca, Saudi Arabia. He was from a Long Island town, ten minutes from my mom's house. What a small world, I thought. I told him that I lived in Abu Dhabi, which I thought might be a good starting point. I have always felt that the entry point of these conversations is so important in expressing intention and motivation. I went on to explain that I was doing research on the adhan, and building an online soundmap of calls to prayer from mosques around the world. He expressed interest and enthusiasm for the project and wanted to know more. As he was also from the United States, I felt he would have a similar cultural reference point to me, which motivated how I went on to explain the project.

"I am trying to provide a more nuanced window into Islam through sound with the hope of countering much of the Islamophobic sentiment that I feel in the U.S."

He nodded. "I am hoping that each adhan I record will carry unique sonic characteristics from the place where I am recording," I continued.

I went on about how before doing some online research, I wasn't sure whether or not there would be an active Muslim community in Iceland and was excited to find this mosque online. Ismaeel explained that there was an active Muslim community, and in fact, there were two mosques in Reykjavik, despite the community being small with somewhere around 1,000 people in total. He explained the reason for the two mosques was due to a division in the way people wanted the communities to be administered and organized, and were not religious in nature.

I asked Ismaeel what brought him to Iceland and about his journey to Mecca from Long Island. He told me that he had wanted to be an Imam for a long time, and he was in the process of studying in Mecca. He was spending Ramadan in Iceland, serving as a Ramadan Imam during the holy month. The Félag Múslima Á Íslandi has several community members who have scholarly backgrounds in Islam and who take turns leading prayers at the mosque. In essence, it is a community-run mosque that has visiting Imams. He asked me to wait for a moment then went into the prayer hall and discussed the request with a few people. He came out and explained that it would be fine for us to record the call to prayer, but that we would be requested to wear headscarves in the prayer room. I asked if it would be okay for my friends to join, and he agreed.

I went back out to the hallway where Heidi and Guðrún had been waiting, and explained what I had learned. The Imam scavenged around the office for headscarves that would appropriately cover us in the prayer room. He then told me that he felt it would be most interesting if one of their congregants who often recited the adhan would be the one to do so on this day. He went on to explain that the man he had in mind was white Icelandic, and the resonance and tonality of more traditional Icelandic music would be present in his recitation of the adhan, making it more representative of Iceland for the soundmap project. The Icelandic man, Brother Oli, agreed, and we all filed into the prayer room and sat on chairs in the back. Ismaeel offered that it was fine for us to take photographs as well.

I took the Sony PCM recorder out of my bag and connected my headphones. As prayer time drew nearer, more people filed into the room. The Icelandic muezzin moved toward the mihrab. We were speaking in hushed tones about the prayer room and the experience. I was aiming to capture the very first word of the adhan; this is incredibly important to my practice of recording, and every adhan on the soundmap meets this requirement. I noted that the muezzin was to begin soon and we all quieted. Brother Oli stood quietly for a moment in front of the wooden domed mihrab at the front of the prayer room, which faced qiblah—the direction of Mecca—and he placed his hands cupped over his ears and began the recitation. The adhan was beautiful and unique, like none I had heard before (figure 6.1 and recording 8).

Reykjavik, Iceland, 2017

Figure 6.1   Prayer Room in the Félag Múslima Á Íslandi, Iceland.

IMAM ISMAEEL BY ISMAEEL MALIK

Imam Ismaeel Malik was the Ramadan Imam for the Félag Múslima Á Íslandi in 2017. Next is a contribution he has written to this book at my request after I had shared with him the chapter on Iceland. This is Ismaeel's own account of our exchanges that Ramadan and his feelings about the soundmap of the Islamic call to prayer.

The summer of 2017 was extraordinarily special for me in many ways. It marked a high point in my career as the Ramadan Imam in the official, state-recognized mosque of Iceland's serene and cozy capital, Reykjavik. It

Recording #8   Félag Múslima Á Íslandi, Reykjavik, Iceland.

was my fifth summer serving, so by then I had been well acclimated to the community and my responsibilities. Being the imam, even if only seasonal as in my case, of the main mosque in the capital city of any country is usually an honor left for only the most experienced, usually senior scholars. Through an almost transcendent twist of fate and the whole "being in the right place at the right time" phenomenon best described in Malcom Gladwell's *Outliers*, somehow, I found myself blessed with a highly fulfilling job in a country hosting\ some of the most scenic nature in the world.

While those who return home after vacationing in Iceland will never stop blabbering on and on about the uniquely mesmerizing nature they witnessed, the incomparably refreshing water they enjoyed drinking, and the purest air they have ever inhaled, for me there is a lot more to Iceland that is often left out. The Icelandic language is such a soothing language to hear; it reminds me of the chirping of birds in the early morning. The people of Iceland are genuine and have a unique and uplifting sense of comedy. The most overlooked part of the Icelandic experience, however, is the almost primordial drive that guided people to move to or visit such a distant and foreign island in the first place. Now, I'm not talking about your average tourists who chose to visit Iceland because it'll get 'em more likes on Insta. I'm talking about the Israeli professor who entered my office asking me about how we fast when we have over 22 hours of sunlight in the summer. Or the Shiite Imam who, after randomly strolling into my office and enjoying some cookies and tea with me, told me how he wished more Sunni Imams would be more like me in their appreciation of the nuances of Islamic Studies and how academically interconnected we all are. Or the upbeat young British woman on vacation who celebrated Eid with our community instead of with her own back home in the UK. "When you meet anyone here, ask them how they got here. Ask them *why* they decided to come here. Their adventures are the craziest things you will ever hear," Brother Oli said to me one day during my first Ramadan back in July of 2013. Gosh, was he right! Thus, for me, one of the best perks of being an imam in Iceland is simply sitting in my office, hearing that knock on the door, not knowing what new adventurous story I am to expect, and excitingly anticipating the *how* and *why* that brought the searching soul knocking on my door.

The *why* that drove Diana Chester and her team to visit our mosque that summer afternoon was particularly inspiring. I remember my mind oscillating between "they're journalists" and "they're converts to Islam" as they approached. When Diana began explaining her project to me, I couldn't help but recall reading, about eight years earlier, Robert Fisk's assertion that "journalists are the foot soldiers of the truth." By highlighting the organic and simple nature of our call to prayer, Diana was essentially combating the rampant Islamophobic rhetoric stereotyping Muslim rites of worship as something exotically sinister. I was particularly moved how someone who isn't a practitioner of our faith appreciates the artistic and social aspects of the adhan and has ventured far and wide in an effort to depict it in a truly remarkable uniting yet pluralistic audio tapestry. Acknowledging that the adhan Diana and her team would record tonight would represent Iceland auditorily, I decided to choose a muezzin whose performance would musically characterize and embody the Icelandic experience of Islam, and the Muslim experience of Iceland. I knew Brother Oli would do both experiences justice because every time he performed the adhan, I could *feel* both experiences. Brother Oli began chanting in his signature chord/mode that never fails to transpose me to *Esjan* and all its grandeur. I could hear his long saga journeying from Iceland to North Africa to Ireland to his conversion to Islam in the distances between the notes he vocalized. Diana had traveled so far to discover this hidden gem, and I was honored to be of assistance in this momentous and historic experience of adding Iceland to the auditory Muslim tapestry.

"There's something in common between everyone who ends up in Iceland some way or another—they are searching for more. They are not afraid of adventure," Brother Ragnar had told me. As Diana and I conversed a little more about ourselves, we were both pleasantly surprised to discover how our life paths were a lot closer than we had imagined. When I told her I'm from Long Island, I wasn't expecting she'd ask, "whereabouts?" "Well, Suffolk County," I respond. When that wasn't sufficient enough, I had realized I was in the presence of someone who clearly has some sort of connection to Strong Island. "Around the Stony Brook/Lake Grove area, that's where I grew up," I said, this time a little more excited. She went on to tell me how her mom's house was only ten minutes away! Additionally, she told me she lived in the UAE, and 2017 would be my second to last year living in Saudi Arabia. I remember thinking to myself, "We never met on Long Island, we didn't even meet in the Middle East (my sister used to live in Dubai so I would visit a couple of times), but it was Iceland where we were meant to first meet." Ragnar was right. We both were clearly adventurous people—world travelers—and Iceland was the perfect host facilitating our meeting and discussion of our mutual love for the art of the adhan.

Chapter 7

A Method for Recording

John Cage's composition *4'33"* is a three-movement composition which instructs the musician or musicians to refrain from playing their instrument(s) for the duration of the piece. Cage's composition is about listening, about reception, and about challenging perceptions of what a composition is. The acoustics of space and noise of place play a critical role in what the audience hears at a performance of *4'33"*, and as a result, the piece is as much about Cage's compositional instructions as it is about an audience's assumptions and expectations of what listening is. *4'33"* becomes about the performer and the audience in the performance space at the moment of the performance, them moving in their seats uncomfortably responding to the silence, the resulting sounds the audience makes in this response, and the way these sounds are heard through the resonance of the physical environment. The field recordings of the adhan on the soundmap can be likened to performances of Cage's *4'33"* in that the instructions for recitation of the adhan—like Cage's composition—are the same for each muezzin, yet the resulting recordings of the adhan are different each time. This is to say that field recordings of the adhan are as much about the recitation as they are about the environment in which they are recorded.

Not only do recordings have the ability to capture an indiscriminate snapshot of an environment, but they can also capture the interaction of the physical environment and the sounds within it. Another way of saying this is that a recording is a story told through the way sound is reflected within a particular environment. When reciting the adhan, the muezzin utilizes his vocal cords, which vibrate to create resonant frequencies, which are then heard or amplified over a loudspeaker. Those same resonances and vibrations, in the form of sound waves, reflect off of buildings, sidewalks, and the urban landscape. Frequencies resonating in large open fields sound different from those amplified in densely packed spaces where structures, people, and vehicles serve as surfaces off which the sound waves can bounce. The recordings of the live adhan therefore capture the resonances of the everyday life of a place through the way the sound of the adhan reflects off of the people and objects in a given community. This makes a recording in the mountains sound very different from one in the city.

Recording the adhan requires a level of preparation, as so much of the process hinges on timing and access. As an audio engineer, I go into the field with my recording equipment, singularly focused on how to make the best quality recording. I am thinking about the sonic environment of a place, the wind, the ambient sounds, my equipment, and the quality of the resulting recording. I am checking the battery level and presets of the audio recorder, and double checking that I am ready to record at the hit of a button. In order to be sure that I am prepared for the challenges I may face in the field and to increase my chances of successfully recording the adhan, I try to plan out each field visit in advance. Typically, I begin by looking up the location of the mosque I will visit, along with the call to prayer times for the geography of that place on the day of the visit. If my visit is to a country or within a culture with which I am not familiar, I will do background research specifically on the orientation and reception of the Islamic community in that place.

Prayer times differ daily and are based on geographic location, as the times are dictated by the rising and setting of the sun. It is also the case that while some mosques follow the prayer timing schedule precisely, others do not. I have noticed a trend in many countries where the Jumu'ah (Friday) Prayer is often held at a fixed time every Friday, regardless of the actual prayer time. The Jumu'ah Prayer is the one prayer each week where Muslims are religiously compelled to pray at the mosque. It has been explained to me that the uniform time is to help streamline the prayer and to make it easier for people, especially those coming from work, to participate.

While visiting the State of Florida, I attempted to record the adhan in two different cities along its West coast. In both instances, the mosques did not sound the adhan, and instead had a sign on the door saying that they hold Jumu'ah prayers on Friday. My takeaway was that in some communities especially those that cater to a wider geographic region or where there are fewer Muslims, Friday is a day when everyone gathers at the mosque for prayer, and in some cases, the mosque or musallah, a prayer space, may only be open for Jumu'ah prayers. This reminds me of my father's family mosque, which has a tiny community and holds prayer only on major holidays, in part because they must bring in a visiting Imam to lead the prayers, and community members must often travel distances to attend.

The next step in my process is to travel to the mosque where I intend to record. If possible, I do this at least a day before I plan to record. However, in many instances, I am in a geography only for one day, in which case, I leave myself a buffer of time between when I arrive and when the adhan is meant to sound. Once I arrive at the mosque, my primary goals are to meet someone from the community, explain my intentions, and determine if the adhan will be amplified, if it will be recited inside the mosque, or if it may not be recited at all. To achieve this, I use some basic observational skills like looking at the facade of the mosque to see if there are any speakers that seem to be permanently installed, or by asking people who may be affiliated with the community. If I do not see any speakers outside or if I want to record from inside the mosque, I will find the main office or the women's prayer room entrance and go inside to ask about the timing for the next adhan, as well as permission to record. All of these preliminary steps impact the resulting conditions in which I record, and often determine whether or not I am successful in recording the adhan.

During a trip to Philadelphia, Pennsylvania, I traveled to the As-Sunnah An-Nabawiyyah Mosque in Germantown to record the adhan. I showed up early to the brick storefront mosque on the main road of the town. There were three doors, two labeled Entrance Brother and one labeled Entrance Sister. I was hesitant to go inside as I did not see anyone go in or out. I could not see inside the building, but I also didn't see anyone outside who seemed affiliated with the mosque, so I stood outside and waited. I investigated the facade for speakers but didn't see any, so I determined the mosque did not amplify the adhan. I also observed that the immediate community surrounding the mosque seemed largely Muslim; there were boys and men in white dishdasha on the street, and women in hijabs, as well as many storefronts with Arabic writing.

A woman around my age wearing a hijab walked by me, and I asked her if she knew if the adhan would sound outside the mosque or only inside. She told me that the adhan would sound right outside momentarily, and she pointed to the sidewalk in front of the mosque between two of the entry doors. "Right there," she said. I was confused since I didn't see any speakers or hear the click of the amplification system being turned on, another key sound I listen for when recording, but I continued to stand outside the mosque and turned my recorder on in preparation.

A young man came out from one of the doors and asked if I was waiting for someone. I told him I was waiting for the adhan. The muezzin walked out from the same door shortly after the younger man and stood in front of the mosque facing outward toward the street—the direction of Mecca—placing his fingertips around his ears with his palms framing his face and pointing toward one another. There without any microphone, he recited the most beautiful adhan out into the street and into the community. I had not before that day seen a muezzin recite the adhan in the street, so I didn't know to expect it. Because I asked the young woman from the community about the timing and location of the adhan, and because these exchanges created a comfort in me to stand outside the mosque and wait, I was standing just a few feet from the muezzin when he recited the adhan. As a result, the recording was reflective of the acoustic recitation and the sounds of street life. Once the muezzin began, I used my body to create sonic isolation between the loud street sounds of buses and cars driving past behind me, and the muezzin in front of me, so that the adhan would be clear and audible in the recording (recording 9).

These moments before and after the adhan begins impact the resulting recording. They often determine whether or not I will be successful in recording the adhan, but also give me a preliminary understanding of the place I am visiting as an outsider, a place that is usually new to me. The process I highlighted earlier, and the steps I take when preparing to record an adhan, support the journey of each visit and each resulting recording. Each step of the process impacts the recording and plays a role in helping me, the recordist, understand the context in which I am recording. My method keeps me curious and observant, as well as aware of the community I am visiting, and what my visit and request to record the adhan asks of that community. This method keeps me aware of how I am received and perceived, of how I introduce and explain my visit, and about how I participate in a community for the period of time in which I am there.

My method and process have evolved over time as I have learned more about Islam and more about what it means to visit a Muslim community. The more knowledge and experience I have doing this research, the more my practice evolves and changes. This method has aided me in learning about the places I visit and has taught me a lot about myself as a field recordist and ethnographer. It has forced me to get better at speaking to people, often strangers, about the work I am doing, and to answer questions about my motivation and intentions for the project. One of the questions I still ponder about

Recording #9   Masjid As-Sunnah An-Nabawiyyah, Philadelphia, Pennsylvania, United States.

this method includes how to articulate my ethnographic research and creative practice in a way that honors the complexity of each, and the interconnectivity of my approach.

I aim to capture recordings of the adhan with as little artifact of my presence as possible. I attempt to capture sounds of the place, ambient aspects of the environment, the people, animals, and vehicles within it, but try to avoid recording myself. I am experienced at being quiet when recording and controlling my breath, but what I can't control is other people talking to me, asking me about what I am doing, about the equipment, and so on. I am completely focused on recording the adhan, but for onlookers particularly those who regularly come to the mosque to pray, seeing someone with an audio recorder may be of interest to them, which easily and often leads to conversation. I try at all costs to avoid these unanticipated conversations happening during the adhan, but I am not always successful. And sometimes this means that I am not successful in capturing the adhan without a discussion happening directly over it, which has often meant I must return later on, or another day to record. In my unedited sound files from these visits, you can hear conversations I have had with people in or around the mosque about what I am doing. Usually, these conversations occur up until five minutes before the adhan sounds, when I try to move to a more secluded space to record, or I leave my recorder setup and I move away from it so that any conversation I have is more distant from the microphones.

Through these case studies, I attempt to show the process of being an artist and ethnographer conducting research about the Muslim communities I have visited. I use written text, imagery, and sound recordings to open a door into another place and invite you in. Most importantly, I share some of the context of these places, my experience visiting each community, and how the relationship between these two factors inform the recordings I have made, each of which serves as a translation of the adhan.

Chapter 8

Florence, Italy, 2017

The first time I visited Italy was in 2014 on a family vacation in celebration of my mother's sixtieth birthday. At that time, I was living in Abu Dhabi and flew to Florence to meet my family who had flown in from New York. My mother had rented an old Tuscan farmhouse where she, my stepdad, my brother, and I stayed for two weeks, using a tiny rental car to make daily excursions throughout the region.

There was an old piano in the Tuscan farmhouse. The keys were worn, and, in some cases, the ivory tops of the wooden keys were missing altogether. The piano was severely out of tune, likely as the result of the cold weather seeping through the stone wall it was placed against, and the contrasting humidity accompanying the warmer days. This fluctuation, coupled with extended periods of not being tuned, made an out-of-tune piano inevitable.

While my brother was able to escape excessive family time to the outdoor table and chairs where he prepared daily for his Bar Association exam, I decided I would escape into the piano. I spent the first few days just getting to know the piano. I would sit down on the wooden bench, punch out a few notes, test out the pedals, and get a feel for how it liked to be played. On the fifth day of our stay, while my mom excitedly cooked up fresh kale that she had collected from the farmers' market, I began composing a piece that became the musical backdrop to our trip.

The tune began like most that I had attempted to compose on piano since the two lessons I had at the age of thirteen. It was a musical number that required me to pound on some keys and softly play others. I leaned into the broken notes, out of tune sounds, and creaks and squeaks of the tool at my disposal, and with vigor, played the song I was composing, over and over again. Later on, when renaming the saved audio files off of the Sony PCM recorder I had brought on the trip, I decided to call the song the Tuscany Song. This proved helpful in allowing me to find it years later among the many unfiled documents on my computer.

The song was inspired by the mystery of the stolen cookies. I was out with my mom while my brother and stepfather were home for the day. Later in the evening after dinner, I remembered the cookies I had bought from the supermarket the day before, and thought it would be nice to have them with tea. But the cookies were mysteriously missing from the bag in my room, and no one seemed to know where they might have gone. The lyrics go something like this, "Did you go into my room and snoop through my bag? No, I was sleeping while you were away. Did you go into the room to find the cookies I had? No, I was snoozing while you were away." And so on.

There is this funny thing that happens, when as adults we spend time within our family, and regress to family dynamics of our childhood. My brother and I are champs at doing this, and to my mother's dismay, family vacations are the perfect breeding ground to help us get right back into our old habits of teasing, taunting, and jeering, not to mention poking fun at our parents' expense.

Several years later, I moved back to New York from the Middle East to work for a tech startup in Brooklyn, New York. My friend and former colleague, Lauren, had also left the Middle East for a job in Florence, where she was able to practice her Italian, visit with extended family, eat amazing food, and mentor young American students on their semester abroad. In April of 2017, I took a vacation to see Lauren in Florence. I flew from New York to Milan and traveled by train from Milan to Florence. I arrived on a Wednesday.

We spent Wednesday catching up and went out to an amazing dinner, where Lauren got eggplant parmigiana, which I wished I had gotten, after which we walked back to her apartment and I passed out early for the night. The next day, I explored Florence on my own and took some time to research Islamic culture and mosques in the city. I had imagined there must be mosques in Florence, but I wasn't sure if they were easily accessible within the city center. As it turned out, there was a mosque within walking distance of Lauren's apartment. From my preliminary internet research, I learned that Florence's Muslim population was around 30,000 people, while their mosques, of which there were three, could not accommodate even 1,000 people at a time. As a result, the leaders of the Muslim community had met with the city council to try and get approval for a larger mosque within the city center that would properly accommodate the community.

At the time of my visit, the discussion between the Muslim community leaders and the city council was still pending, and while it was being reported in the papers that the city council said they would work to find a solution, there was a strong precedent set by Lombardy, a northern region of Italy, referred to as the "anti-mosque" law. In Lombardy, there were laws passed that made it extremely difficult for religions not officially recognized by the country to get approval to build places of worship. Additionally, there were specifications in architectural requirements that made the building of minarets, or "slender towers," impossible to pass through building code in the region.

That Friday, Lauren and I took a walk to Masjid Al-Taqwa and the Comunita Islamica Di Firenze E Toscana for the Jumu'ah Prayer. I packed my Sony PCM recorder and DSM microphones in the hope that we would be able to record the adhan. Lauren had never heard the adhan sound in Florence and wasn't sure if it was amplified outside the mosque. It was a beautiful day, sunny and cool, as we made our way toward the Loggia del Pesce, or Fish's Lodge, the major landmark near where the mosque was located. The Islamic finder said the prayer time would be at 12:30 pm. We quickly walked down the uneven cobblestone streets of Florence. We were running late. As we approached the mosque on Borgo Allegre, we walked past a children's playground on our right, where mats had been laid out across the entire fenced-in area. We could see several worshippers picking up their prayer mats and leaving the playground. There were men who followed behind them, picking up the mats that had been laid down in an overlapping fashion one on top of another, covering the playground floor.

I noticed that the worshippers in the playground had their mats facing toward the front door of the mosque, across the street, which was also the direction of Mecca, the direction that Muslims orient themselves while praying. The mosque was on a small residential street, at ground level, in a four-story yellow building that had green shutters on the windows of the upper-level apartments. The mosque itself was made up of what looked like two separate storefronts. The storefront on the left, with its protective metal draw-down gate, had a blue and white sign above the door marked by the number 66, with the following inscribed in Arabic and Italian, "Comunita Islamica Di Firenze E Toscana-Islamic Community of Florence and Tuscany." The storefront to the right was of a similar shape and size and had a matching sign above its rolling gate, which read Masjid Al-Taqwa in Arabic and in English transliteration, with a graphic of a dome and minaret mosque flanking the text, and the number 64 marked on the side.

As we turned the corner, I could smell the aroma of shawarma being sold out of milk crates strapped to the back of bicycles, and chai (tea) being tipped out of large steel thermoses into plastic cups. There were hundreds of men filling the street. I presumed they had just finished praying and were enjoying lunch after prayer.

The exterior of the mosque looked just like the street shops beside it on either side. There were no minarets or symbols that made the space stand out as a mosque, aside from the signage above the door. The interior of the masjid looked more like a large open room, which was once a storefront of some kind with folding privacy doors that could close. I didn't go inside but got a decent glimpse of it from across the street. The community center entrance had a single door, with people frequently coming in and out, and a large glass window pane on the left with white floor-to-ceiling blinds. I wondered if the timetable I was following from online was wrong, and in fact we had just missed the Jumu'ah prayer, as it seemed. Lauren went to buy a Shawarma and I crossed the street toward the mosque.

I made my way to the community center door, where several men were standing in the threshold blocking my view of the inside. I was trying to see if the inside might have had the mosque office, or if by entering I would be inadvertently walking inside the prayer room. A gentleman in the doorway saw me looking about and moved to one side, gesturing for me to enter. The inside of the community center reminded me of the headmistress's office in some of the government schools I had worked at in Bangalore, India. Along the side of the room with the blinds and the door was a bookshelf overflowing with books, and across the room from the bookshelf was a very large metal desk, with a stately red upholstered desk chair, the kind in which the most important person in the organization sits. Behind the desk were several wood and glass lock cabinets, with skeleton key holes, and on the desk a variety of papers, writing implements, and books. On the left wall, nestled between the bookshelves and the large desk, was a red fabric–colored couch, with wooden arms. And on the far right behind the desk was a narrow doorway with no door, which led somewhere I could not see.

"Excuse me," I said. "Can I speak with someone about recording the adhan?"

An older man with a skull cap and glasses smiled at me. He then said something, in Italian, to the man who had earlier gestured for me to enter the doorway. The older man looked back toward me and gestured for me to sit on the red couch. He walked through the small doorway behind the desk, as though to look for someone who spoke English. I took a seat on the red couch, and felt myself being very still, trying to take in my surroundings and the community, and to figure out a bit about the context before someone came back through the doorway. After all, I knew next to nothing about this community, aside from what I had read on the internet. I started looking more closely at some of the books on the shelf and noticed that many were in Arabic and some were in Italian. The men in the threshold walked outside as if to give me my privacy, and I found myself alone in the Islamic center office. Behind the desk, in one of the glass cabinets, I noticed robes like those I had seen worn by imams in other mosques.

After a few minutes passed, I remembered the objective that had brought me to the mosque—recording the adhan. I rifled through my small backpack to pull out the Sony PCM recorder in the event that we had not missed the adhan, and it was still to come. Lauren was still outside eating her shawarma, and I was close to the prayer room, giving me the best chance of recording an interesting adhan. I powered on the recorder and placed my white earbuds in the headphone jack and then into my ears. I monitored the room through the headphones and hit the record button just in case the adhan was to sound. I looked around the room again and out the door toward the street, where there were still many people milling about. I wanted to take out my DSM microphones that were packaged in a black zippered case, almost resembling a 1990s CD wallet that would hold fifty compact discs and be placed under the passenger seat of your car.

Growing up right outside of New York City, I was raised to always be aware of my surroundings, and to be engaged with the space and people near me. Traveling and conducting research have taught me to always be aware of how my presence may be seen or interpreted by the communities I visit. In this case, I was in a largely immigrant community of Muslims in a country that did not officially recognize Islam, during a time when there was tension between the community and the city council about building new spaces of worship. I was a foreigner to this community, an English-speaking woman with fair skin and dark hair, visually aligning me with the Italian majority community of Florence. I was sitting in what I believed to be the imam's office and was not entirely sure if my homemade DSM microphones would cause alarm.

The DSM microphones were home-built by an engineer in the United States, who placed them on either end of a headband that was meant to be placed on top of the head much like fuzzy earmuffs. The two microphones, which sat at either side of the headband covering the ears, were wrapped in a dark mesh material tied off with colored heat shrink (black for left and red for right), making the whole setup appear as headphones to the untrained eye. However, I was aware that the homemade quality of the microphones could make them appear odd in certain contexts, which lead me to sometimes avoid taking them out. I stopped the Sony recorder and connected the DSM microphones to the line input. I selected a phantom power option from the menu and turned the microphone gain all the way to zero. I placed the DSM microphones over my head and sat them just in front of my ears, inside of which I was wearing earbuds. I then slowly dialed up the microphone gain until I could hear the chatter of the men from outside the door in my headphones. Out of the left DSM microphone, I could hear the sounds of people speaking and praying coming from behind the wall against which the imam's robes were hanging.

The older gentleman with the spectacles and skull cap came back through the doorway with a younger man in a suit. The younger man said hello in English and asked how he could help. This was the imam. I explained why I was there, that I was visiting Florence, and was hoping to record the adhan for an ongoing project where I collected recordings of the adhan from mosques around the world. I explained that my mission was to highlight the nuance and diversity of the call to prayer through an online soundmap. He welcomed me to the mosque and told me a bit about the community, including the most obvious point, that they had so many worshippers that they overflowed into the neighboring playground. He also told me that on Fridays, they held two different prayer sessions to accommodate the number of people who wanted to worship. I guess unlike Abu Dhabi, where it is expected that worshippers will spill out onto the street and stop traffic during the Jumu'ah Prayer, in Florence, permission was needed to use the playground for overflow, which by the looks of it, was larger than the interior prayer room, but still insufficient to accommodate all of the Friday worshippers.

The imam went on to explain that when I arrived, the first prayer time had just concluded, and in ten minutes, they would begin the second prayer time, which was held only inside the prayer room of the masjid, and not on the playground. I asked if they would again recite the adhan for this second prayer, and he told me that they would. I asked if they sounded the adhan inside only, and he told me that they did sound the adhan outside as well. He asked me where I was from, and I explained that I grew up in the United States and had spent the prior six years living in Abu Dhabi. He told me he was from Palestine and had been in Italy for twenty-some odd years. I asked if many of the congregants were from Palestine as well, and he said they were from all over. He welcomed me to record the adhan and excused himself to prepare for the prayer. I thanked him as he walked back through the threshold into the back room.

I took the recorder and microphones and placed them in my backpack and quickly went outside to search for Lauren. I asked if she would be willing to record the adhan from outside the mosque on my phone while I stayed inside the office and recorded the adhan from there. I stepped back into the office, which was empty, plopped myself on the couch, and quickly placed the DSM headband on my head and earphones in my ears, turned the recorder on and hit play in order to not miss the start of the adhan.

My heart was racing. I was excited. I was thankful for the conversation with the imam and his kindness, and I was excited to be recording the adhan in a new community and sonically experiencing the sounds of the call to prayer in a new place and culture.

Through the headphones, I heard a lot of chatter coming from the doorway between the imam's office and what I now realized was the prayer room. At this point, I had figured out that the two storefront entrances connected in the back. I moved closer to the threshold with the recorder to see if I could see the prayer room, which I could not. When it began, I could hear the chatter quiet down as the muezzin began his recitation. In his breath after the first verse, I quickly rolled the microphone gain dial-up to try and make out the adhan more clearly. Because of the wall between myself and the prayer room, the sound was very muffled. I still was not happy with what I was hearing through the headphones, and at his next breath, I removed one of my earbuds to listen to the sound as it resonated in the office doorway, where I was standing. It was just as I was hearing it in the recording, muffled and distant, as though the adhan was being recited behind two concrete walls. I remained still and focused throughout the adhan, and when it had finished, I switched off the recorder and placed the microphones, headphones, and recorder in my backpack as I made my way back out to the street.

"Did you hear it out here?" I asked Lauren.

Figure 8.1   Masjid Al-Taqwa, Florence, Italy.

Chapter 8

Recording #10   Masjid Al-Taqwa, Florence, Italy—Jumu'ah Adhan.

"Yes, it was soft but it was coming out of megaphone-shaped speakers that I think are sitting just behind the gate in the playground. I pressed myself up against the gate and stuck my arm through to be as close to where I heard the sound coming from as I could."

"Do you think you got a clear recording?" I asked.

"Yes, I think so. There was street noise, but I could hear it really clearly and imagine that the recorder captured it as clearly," she said.

We looked at each other and smiled. I could tell that this was not Lauren's typical Friday afternoon in Florence, and we were both having a great time. We got chai from one of the tea bicycle vendors and stood around the mosque for a while longer, taking in the atmosphere, the community, and listening to people speaking Arabic, Italian, Urdu, and other languages native to the worshippers, before turning the corner and continuing onward back to Lauren's office (figure 8.1 and recording 10).

Chapter 9

Christchurch, New Zealand, 2019

March 15, 2019. A BBC alert flashes across the screen of my phone. The three-line notification reads, "Breaking News, many casualties feared as police warn an active shooter is at large after an attack on a mosque in Christchurch, New Zealand." One month later, I was in Christchurch visiting the Al Noor Mosque. I went on a Friday morning before Jumu'ah Prayer, and the scene outside the mosque was striking. There were flowers, signs, and tributes scrawled on paper and fabric, lining the gate from one end to the other. It was a vigil for the victims of the attack. There were police officers with large guns, standing outside the main gate of the mosque. A man with a beard, who was wearing a skull cap, was confirming the identities of people who were driving up to the gate in cars, so that the police would wave them through to the interior parking lot. I approached the man in the skull cap. "As-salām alaykum," I said. A standard Arabic greeting, which literally means peace be upon you. I use this greeting not only to say I come in peace, but as a way for me to say that I am not a foreigner to Islam and that I have some understanding, can speak a little Arabic, and respect the community. The man responded, "Wa alaykum as-salām" [And upon you be peace]. I asked if the mosque was open to the public, and he said yes, it is open all day except during a few hours on Friday when it is closed for the Jumu'ah Prayer. I thanked him and returned the following morning.

    The guards were still there on Saturday, but this time I was allowed to enter through the gate. I walked toward the main door of the mosque. It was familiar—the same one I had seen on the Facebook livestream a month earlier. Just past the front door, there was a small interior vestibule and beyond that a long corridor which led to the main prayer room. I recognized the corridor from the videos I had seen on the news, and chills ran down my back. Both the corridor and the prayer room seemed to be under renovation. They both had exposed gray sub-carpet in place of where the carpet had once been. It was later explained to me by a member of the community that all of the carpets had to be replaced due to bloodstains. On my right, before the corridor began, there was a table with brochures, small pamphlets, DVDs, and a guest book. There was also a small box for donations.

I had seen very similar brochures two weeks earlier when I was visiting the Perth Mosque in Western Australia. The Perth Mosque was having an open day barbeque where they invited non-Muslim members of the community to visit the mosque and learn about Islam over lemonade and sausages. There, by contrast, everyone had been welcomed to walk into the mosque, and there were no guards or barriers to doing so. In the back of the bustling interior courtyard of the Perth Mosque, where the grills were set up and the line for food snaked, there were informational tables piled high with pamphlets and books displayed on stands. The members of the community stationed at these tables were eager to talk to visitors about Islam, its tenets, and the religion. They handed out free pamphlets and materials, as well as the Saheeh International Qur'an, a small, thick mustard yellow softcover book, containing a complete English translation of the Qur'an. Later that afternoon, there was a large Haka performed on the main road outside the mosque. The Haka, a traditional cultural dance of the indigenous Māori people of New Zealand, was planned in honor of the victims of the Christchurch shooting.

Figure 9.1 Perth Mosque, Australia.

Christchurch, New Zealand, 2019

Recording #11   Perth Mosque, Australia—Dhuhr Adhan.

It attracted a large crowd of onlookers who watched and cheered to fight Islamophobia and to support the Muslim community in Perth, as well as those in Christchurch, and around the world (figure 9.1 and recording 11).

As I was thumbing through the pamphlets in the empty Al-Noor Mosque, I noticed a room behind the table and made my way there. It was a women's prayer room with some books, chairs, and places to hang your jacket. I heard someone enter the mosque and walked back out to the corridor. There I met several members of the Al-Noor community, a visiting imam from Malaysia, and two Muslim men from South Africa who, like me, were there to give their love and condolences, and to share messages of love and support from people who could not themselves visit the mosque. We talked in small groups

Figure 9.2   Al Noor Mosque, Christchurch, New Zealand.

Recording #12 Al Noor Mosque, Christchurch, New Zealand—Dhuhr Adhan.

for a while about life, about love and support, about the community in New Zealand, and about how everyone came together. More people entered the mosque and the prayer time neared. The muezzin recited the adhan, and with his permission, I recorded it (figure 9.2 and recording 12).

Chapter 10

Recording as Translation

People have asked me why I go through all the trouble to record the adhan live rather than leveraging existing recordings. I can understand the question given that it is possible to hear a wide array of adhan recitations from around the world through streaming services on the internet, call to prayer alarm clocks, and on mobile phone adhan apps. And of course, it can be costly and time-consuming to travel to each destination to record the adhan. I have come up with two answers to this question, the latter of which has formed more recently, though I believe it is one of the central purposes of the research methodology that binds these pages together.

My first response is that a recording of a thing is not the same as the thing itself, an idea I will return to throughout the book. The live recordings I make of the call to prayer are not the call to prayer but can perhaps be considered a type of translation of the call to prayer. These translations include the daily sounds of life from where the recordings are made, the people who are present in that place at that specific moment in time, aspects of the landscape, the muezzin's recitation, breath, pitch, and style, and when present, the amplification mechanism used to transmit the adhan. They also include the characteristics of the room or building where the adhan is recited, the buildings and structures surrounding the mosque from where the adhan is amplified, weather conditions at the time of the recitation, and the presence of the recordist making a record of it all.

A recording of a thing is not the same as the thing itself. Think of a press conference where twenty journalists are swarming with their cameras and microphones around the featured speaker to broadcast a event live. For this example, let's assume the journalists are all in similar proximity to the person speaking. One camera person has an angle of the left side of the speaker's face, another the right side, and a few are shooting face on. As a result, the light and background behind the speaker look slightly different in each shot, and maybe a different portion of the room is in the camera's frame. All of this may seem negligible, but what if one camera captures the speaker and the person standing to her right, but the shot completely omits anyone standing to her left. That footage on its own becomes a translation of the press conference, a translated visual version of the story, dictated by framing. Similarly, the twenty sound recordings of that press conference will reveal slightly different information. One recording may reveal a cough, a phone ringing in the background, a comment spoken under one's breath, any of which might not be captured on a recording that was taken from a different location, angle, or proximity. Overlay this with differences in the way the operators set the recording devices, how loud or soft their levels were, the quality of the microphones, the direction in which they were pointed, and so on. Each recording is a translation through the specific frame of the recordist and their tools.

My second response is that field recording live and in context involves visiting a community and often meeting the people who live there. Making a field recording is nothing like listening to a recording of the adhan online. It is not simply an act of listening, nor is it an isolated act that can take place on one's computer or phone at home. Recording the adhan live at a mosque involves interacting with people, visiting a community, and learning something, even if small, about one's self, about the people and their community, and them about you. Field recording in a community is a form of ethnographic research, a practice that necessitates exchange, communication, comprehension, and consideration of a sonic vantage point necessarily shaped by that research. One of the factors that makes a field recording a translation is the sonic frame. The sonic frame is determined by the specific and unique choices made by the person recording, which result in the recording sounding the way it does. Our engagement with the places where we record and the people in those places directly affects the story a recording tells.

Through the course of this research project, many recordists, both amateur and those that think about recording more technically and critically, have made contributions to the soundmap. Retrospectively, I have become interested in the experience one has recording the adhan for this project. I wondered if the process of making recordings impacted others the way it impacted me. Which is to ask, how would another describe their experience engaging with a community through the practice of listening and recording the call to prayer? I thought it might be interesting to offer another's experience recording the adhan for the soundmap. Guilherme Menezes and I became acquainted in late 2019, when he responded to a call for the soundmap that I had posted on a field recording Facebook page. I was, at the time, specifically looking for folks who might be interested in recording the adhan in South America, as it was the only continent other than Antarctica without representation on the map. Guilherme was living in Fortaleza, Brazil, at the time and offered to help with the project. The following is his account of visiting Centro Cultural Beneficente Islâmico do Ceará and recording the adhan.

ADHAN RECORDING IN FORTALEZA, CEARÁ, BRAZIL BY GUILHERME MENEZES

My name is Guilherme Menezes. I am a 28-year-old DJ and producer from Teresina, Brazil. My interest in sound recording began when I started researching music philosophy and taking part in artistic residencies. During the residencies, I met people from Brazil, Argentina, and Spain who did field recording and used it as part of their production technique and process. In their work, these artists were raising identity, history, socioeconomic, and environmental issues through the recorded sounds of a moment in time. I saw a call in a field recordings group on Facebook asking for field recordings of the call to prayer and got in contact with Diana. I wanted to participate in the soundmap project because I thought contributing to a worldwide project would be interesting and because I knew very little of Islamic culture and tradition.

On December 6, 2019, I went to the Islamic Cultural Beneficent Center in Fortaleza to get to know the mosque, the people, to talk with them for a while and to record the adhan. I was told over the phone that the adhan is made every day at noon punctually, so I went an hour early to settle into the environment and get some more information. The actual mosque is on the second floor of a two-story building, and some of the community members live on the first floor of the same building. I took photos of the outside structure, and with permission, of the inside space—its cushions, carpets, the al-Qur'an, shoes and sandals left outside, the boxes of books and the vibrant colors of the main room in shades of brown, gold, red, and green (figure 10.1 and recording 13).

One of the first things I noticed was the separation of gender. Men and women coexist in the same communal places, but there were separate rooms for each. I greeted the women with a slight nod, and they answered back. Then, the men invited me into their kitchen and offered me some coffee, and to have a seat. They were of different ages, from different geographic regions and religious backgrounds, and all found in Islam comfort, identification, and

Figure 10.1 Centro Cultural Beneficente Islâmico do Ceará, Fortaleza, Brazil. *Source:* Image courtesy of Guilherme Menezes.

devotion. They were very curious about my visit to their mosque and asked how I got there. They told me that people from various academic fields including historians, anthropologists, sociologists, and philosophers had already visited them for research purposes. I explained to them a little bit about the project I was participating in and the reason I wanted to record their call to prayer. I did not have the opportunity to talk to any of the women, aside from them telling me the location of the room where the adhan was going to be recited.

In the main room, where the Qur'an was open on a pedestal, there were some people already praying silently. I had a conversation with Y, the person

Recording #13 Centro Cultural Beneficente Islâmico do Ceará, Fortaleza, Brazil. Recorded by Guilherme Menezes.

I talked to on the phone earlier. He is a young man from Salvador, Bahia, originally from a Catholic family, who decided to live in Fortaleza to study and convert to Islam. We talked for about fifteen minutes on the nature of the Qur'an, Mohammed, Allah, The Creation, the Bible, God, The Holy Trinity, The Holy Spirit, and other interesting subjects.

J, an even younger man who was sitting next to us, was going to recite the adhan. Our conversation was interrupted by Y, as we were close to the adhan moment. The whole conversation and the call to prayer were recorded with my personal cellphone and closed-ear headphones. It was interesting to witness the reciting of the adhan which was performed in four directions, east, south, north, and west. Everybody in the mosque respected the moment of the recitation with silence, which made it possible to experience the ambiance of the room, which was made up of a low volume static noise from the fan blower and the outside birds' synchronous chirping with J's voice.

It was interesting to hear the differences in timbre and the nuances of volume as J was performing the adhan, and slightly pitch shifting with his voice. As a Brazilian man with Indigenous, Mediterranean European and African origins, I have always had a more distant relationship with Islamic culture. My references for Islam were based in stereotypes depicted on soap operas, famous here in Brazil, high school history books, and literature and poetry like those of Rumi and Shams Tabrizi. Catholic, Afrocentric, and indigenous shamanic rituals are the more common religious practices in South America, where percussive instruments are used along with the voice.

Having the opportunity to record an Islamic call to prayer was a valuable experience for me. It opened my worldview to interesting cultural differences and made me realize that as humans, we all crave spiritual connections. I was very well received at the mosque and welcomed to come back. I was also intrigued by how much can be captured in a moment by a simple recording. It is somewhat like photography or video, where you "freeze" a moment in time and space for eternity to observe and analyze. This recording can be a tool for learning, teaching, or just contemplated by itself, for the memory and emotional connections that it holds.

Chapter 11

Yangon, Myanmar, 2014

While visiting a friend in Myanmar in 2014, I wanted to record the call to prayer at a mosque in Yangon. I had a very basic knowledge about the Muslim community in Myanmar. I understood that they were largely Bengali-speaking people known as Rohingya who had at some point emigrated from present-day Bangladesh, and they lived largely in the Rakhine State of Myanmar. The friend I was visiting worked for an international non-governmental organization (NGO) that was, at the time, doing work with the Rohingya population in Myanmar who were experiencing persecution. She told me stories of how she, a darker-skinned Indian woman, was for safety reasons not allowed to travel for work to some of the key communities they were trying to serve. She explained that her dark skin meant she might be read as Rohingya, which in some parts of Myanmar at that time, meant that she was at higher risk of being the victim of violent attacks from the Buddhist community. I was surprised to learn these details of my friend's work in Myanmar and felt embarrassingly ill-informed. In 2014, the anti-Rohingya sentiment and violence were not commonly reported in global news as it was in 2017, when newspapers and televisions were filled with coverage of the violence and displacement crises faced by the Rohingya people of Myanmar.

    I spent my first three days in Yangon, walking around the city and getting a feel for the architecture, language, and culture while shooting some street photography. I didn't notice any overt violence or bubbling aggression in public, and the people I met, mostly shop keepers, friends and colleagues of my friend, and restaurant folks, were all very nice. A few days into my visit I decided to venture out to record the adhan. I had located a mosque in close walking distance to where I was staying and set out with my Sony PCM recorder and the camera on my phone. This was in an attempt to be as low profile as possible. I imagined that the Muslim community in Yangon was likely on high alert as a result of the violence my friend had told me about.

I arrived at the mosque, a several-story-tall brick building that blended in with all the other buildings on the block. The mosque occupied a corner building and the entrance was around the side of the building from the street on which I approached. In an attempt to get my bearings, I found a spot across the street from the mosque where I stood for a while to observe the building. I noticed a small group of men arrive and then enter the mosque, and a few passersby, but little else. Some of the men who gathered in front of the mosque looked in my direction, and I observed them observing me, but I did not go over to them. There was something inside of me that was nervous about approaching the men outside the mosque. In retrospect, I think I was worried about how to explain my presence to the men outside the mosque. I didn't yet feel comfortable trying to explain my research project, and at a more fundamental level, I wasn't sure I could navigate the language barrier and still communicate my intentions and motivation. I had realized early on in the soundmap project that intention and motivation were very important to me and my process. I was able to identify these within myself, which was critical to my comfort in recording at mosques, my ability to explain the reason for the project, and to believe in its value. On this day, I was not able to fully access this intention and motivation inside myself.

I left my post and walked up and down the small side street staying close to the mosque, waiting for the adhan to sound. It never did. The next day, I returned to the same mosque at a different time. I arrived close to the prayer time and stood in the side street. Again, there was no adhan amplified outside of the mosque. At this point, I thought that perhaps mosques in Myanmar didn't amplify the adhan, a practice I first learned about in Singapore where the government has particular rules governing the playing of religious sounds in the public domain.

The following day, I traveled to the downtown of Yangon, to the Chulia Muslim Dargah Mosque, whose dome and minarets towered above many of the other buildings. The Mosque was a few blocks away from an ornate South Indian Hindu Temple with its colorful pyramid-shaped pier towering in the sky, and directly across the street from the touristy Bogyoke Market. The mosque was on a major artery of the city that was bustling with cars, bikes, buses, people, and sidewalk vendors selling their wares. The mosque shot up high in the sky, a light pink with teal accent trim, topped with a large golden dome and a symphony of golden tipped minarets, all of which glistened in the sun of the day. I crossed the busy street and made my way to the mosque thirty minutes before the Asr adhan was meant to sound.

The architectural front of the mosque, marked by an ornate door on the main road above which a big yellow sign reading Chulia Muslim Dargah

Mosque hung, was sandwiched by shop fronts selling postcards and small soccer balls suspended in mesh netting that lined the street side of the tarp-covered entryways. The closed front doors of the mosque and absence of foot traffic in or out suggested this was not the entrance people used for prayer. I walked around the corner to a side street, which was by contrast very quiet and shaded. There was a similar-looking doorway over which a similar yellow sign hung, across from which there was a makeshift outdoor food stall under two collapsible tents. The two men packing up the food stall, who appeared to be Rohingya, were washing dishes, packing up the chairs, and putting away the temporary cooking facility. I assumed, from my conversations earlier in the week with my friend, that these men might be Bengali speaking, which meant that while I didn't speak Bengali, I could probably communicate with some basic Hindi and that we might understand one another. I approached their tent, physically gesturing toward the men and then across my body toward the mosque with my hands.

"Adhan hain?" I asked? One of the men looked at me with a lack of recognition for what I was saying. "Namaaz hain?" I tried a different word, one I often heard used when I lived in India to refer to prayer. Again, no response.

"Athan, Adhaan?" I repeated with slightly different pronunciations. I saw a look of recognition flash across the face of the man packing away the metal plates.

"Adhaan," he said while pointing to the mosque.

With my index finger, I tapped my wrist, where there was no wristwatch and asked, "kittna time? adhaan time?"

With metal plates still in hand, he turned toward the other man and said something, which led to a short discussion, before he turned back in my direction and said, "Saday teen."

"Saday teen baje?" I asked.

The man nodded. The adhan would be at 3:30 pm. My search on the Islamic Prayer finder that morning had also indicated that the Asr prayer time for that day would be at 3:30 pm. The man who was behind the tent packing away large aluminum cooking vessels now walked toward us. He looked in my direction and asked, "Aap kidhar se hain?"

"US se," I responded, preferring to refer to the United States this way, though I could see he did not recognize the country. "America se." I rephrased, giving into the most commonly understood name for the country where I am from.

The man nodded his head in recognition. "Kya aap Musalmaan hain?" he asked?

This was a question I had become accustomed to being asked when I visited mosques, and one I was still not completely comfortable answering. I am not Muslim. I don't practice Islam nor was I raised in the faith. However, my father was raised Muslim and his parents and family are all Muslim for generations and generations and generations. My heritage both culturally, with regard to language, dress, food, and tradition, and ethnically, tied to ancestral roots in Mongolia, migration through Turkey, and then onward to Central Asia and North America, is all inextricably connected to Islam.

"Mere papa Musalmaan hain," I responded. This is how I would always respond. While this is closer to the truth, and something I could easily say with my basic Hindi language skills, it also wasn't entirely accurate.

I had a great conversation with a Pakistani Canadian friend with whom I worked in Abu Dhabi. I asked him how in Urdu or Hindi, I could express my conundrum when people ask if I am Muslim. I told him that simply saying no, I was not Muslim, didn't feel right, because my reason for doing research on the adhan and visiting mosques felt connected to my heritage and my own search to understand more about Islam through sound, an inroad that was intuitive for me. And yet to say my father was Muslim was also not correct, as he is not a religious person.

"You can say, mere papa Islami khandaan se ta'alluk rakhte hain, which means my father comes from an Islamic background," He offered.

That felt good to me, and it felt true. Now I need to practice saying it so that the next time I find myself in a situation to explain my relationship to Islam in Urdu, I will be ready. Then it dawned on me that while I had before been in many situations where I could explain this narrative in English, I never did, but instead opted to simply explain that I was doing research on the adhan.

Both men nodded their heads, satisfied with my response, and began packing up the rest of their cooking equipment and collapsing the tents. I put one of my headphones into my ear and connected the other end to the audio recorder. I could hear the screeching of old car brakes on the main road, the chatter of children, and the endless footsteps of people walking down the side street. I pushed record so that I would be sure to capture the entire adhan. I stretched the elastic on the fuzzy windscreen over the top of the built-in microphones until it sat correctly around the body of the recorder, connected the small grip attachment for me to hold onto, and waited for the adhan to sound. I walked up and down the side street listening to my own footsteps as I paced, sonically immersed in the street sounds of Yangon—large buses chugging down the high-traffic main street, cars honking, the sounds of sweeping from the two men behind me—sonically observing my surroundings.

As I passed by the main door to the mosque, I waited for people to clear the frame and then clicked a picture which had the name of the mosque inscribed. A man with a skull cap walked past me and my fuzzy windscreen-covered audio recorder and looked at me with what I imagine might have been intrigue and curiosity, or perhaps suspicion. After all, I was out of place in this scene. He yelled something in my direction, which I could hear loudly through the headphones, but did not understand. My head involuntarily looked up in his direction to find him looking right back at me. One of the men from the makeshift restaurant yelled something in his direction, which I did not understand either, but it seemed to satisfy the man with the skull cap, and so he carried on about his business. The adhan began (figure 11.1 and recording 14).

I try to not move once the adhan begins, as I don't want my handling noise, the sound of my clothes ruffling, or my own footsteps to be included in the

Figure 11.1   Chulia Muslim Dargah Mosque, Yangon, Myanmar.

Recording #14   Chulia Muslim Dargah Mosque, Yangon, Myanmar.

recording whenever possible. There were children running around outside the mosque, playing and carefree. Their voices and shrieks are on the recording I made, as are the sounds of the two men clanging together steel pots as they put them away, as are the somewhat distant sounds of the main road, and possibly even the tourists across the street in the market. The adhan ended and I hit stop. Several children had been lingering nearby for a while, this time definitely intrigued and curious as to who I was and what I was doing. Once the adhan ended, I stopped the recording and looked up in the direction of the children. The most brazen girl among them came over and spoke to me in English.

"Hello, what is your name?" she asked.

"Hello, my name is Diana, what is your name," I replied.

She asked me what I was doing. I showed her the audio recorder and played back the recording of the adhan as she listened through my earphones. I hit the record button so that she could hear the sounds we made together through the microphone. She lit up with a huge smile. More of the children gathered around, listened, and asked questions for a while until I eventually made my way back to my friend's apartment.

Chapter 12

Bali, Indonesia, 2017

Wayan was the name of our driver, a nice Balinese man who wore batik button-downs and drove a black Toyota SUV. We first met at the Denpasar airport late on a Wednesday night when Heidi and I flew in from Singapore. He offered us cold beverages, which he kept tucked into a small handheld cooler in the back of the car, the kind we brought on Sunday beach excursions when I was a kid. He safely drove us the hour and fifteen minutes to our hotel in Ubud, an inland jungle area on the Indonesian island of Bali.

When I made the reservation with the hotel for a pickup at the airport, I was told that our driver would be holding a sign outside of the baggage claim with the name of the hotel on it. As Heidi and I exited the baggage claim area through an opaque sliding glass door, we walked into a tiled interior walkway that snaked its way along a stainless-steel banister that at four and a half feet tall served as the separation barrier between the new arrivals to the airport and those that had shown up to receive them. There were at least 200 people standing packed like sardines in uneven chaotic rows going back four and five people deep behind the steel banister. Many had arms jutting out in front of them at varying heights, holding A4-sized paper placards with the name of the hotel they were heading toward, or the name of a guest they were waiting to pick up.

This was a familiar airport arrival scene. At New York's John F. Kennedy Airport, where I fly into when I travel home, there are always people waiting for their loved ones, some with flowers and signs, others holding up babies so that they can see through the crowds, and always men in black suits with laminated signs that have the name of the person they are there to retrieve. At India's Cochin International Airport where I go annually to research a Hindu Festival, in addition to drivers with signs, and the lone boyfriend holding flowers, there are often large families of ten or more waiting to receive one family member who is returning from working or studying overseas. And here at Denpasar airport in Bali, there were rows of Balinese men, all with signs, waiting to pick up guests who they would drive to hotels and resorts around the island.

I felt overwhelmed by the number of signs. Over the years, I had developed a persona, an alter ego, for that moment when I walked through the exit door at the airport. The persona was a combination of calm, collected, and don't fuck with me. I'm sure I first developed it after living in India, when every time I come through an airport or train station, I would be accosted by people, always men, running up to me wanting to help with my bags, or to drive me somewhere in a taxi. I remember one particular instance when several men actually followed me around as I tried to collect my thoughts, figure out what to do and who to trust. I initially learned how to say, taxi nahin chahiye [I don't need a taxi], though that worked with only moderate success. Eventually I learned how to say, mere gari wahaan hai [My car is over there], and then mere driver wahan hai [My driver is over there]. That seemed to get the response I was looking for.

With 200 people and almost as many signs, I was completely taken off guard. I charged out the glass sliding door with my typical persona, confidently looking for the direction of the taxi stand or bus platform and following the way, as though I knew where I was going, with purpose. But to read all those signs with confidence and without my glasses from that fifteen-foot distance just wasn't going to happen. I walked in the direction of the steel banister and methodically scanned the signs starting at the far-right side and back into the crowd. I was struggling to block the "noise" of all of the visual cues, all of the white signs with black letters on them.

"There's your name," Heidi said. That's not possible, I thought to myself without having yet seen the sign. The hotel said the driver would be holding a sign with the name of the hotel on it. I shifted my focus from my methodical scanning to Heidi, who was standing next to me, smiling. She pointed, to a man in the first row, right up against the railing and all the way to the right. The sign read, Ms. Dianna Chester. "Yup, that's us," I said, chuckling inside at the slight misspelling of my name, which conjured memories of the wide variety of misspelled airport name placards I have experienced in my life. I confidently strutted over to the man with the sign, pulling my rolling carry-on behind. The three men I was walking toward all looked at me. I pointed to the sign with my name. Wayan's already-friendly-looking face now became an upturned smile, as he gestured instructions for us to walk around the crowd and off to the left as he disentangled himself from the sardine lines. He disappeared into the back of the crowd, and Heidi and I walked in the direction he pointed. Our path snaked around the duty-free shop, into a narrowing hallway where you would expect to find the bathrooms, and eventually met up with the path where Wayan was waiting. He took one of our bags and we followed him across the street, into an elevator, down a floor, through the parking garage, to the other side of the pay gate, across the main artery road for the airport terminals, and ultimately over a small gulley of flowing water, to where the car was parked. After helping us and our bags into the car, Wayan handed us bottles of water from a small cooler in the back. As we were about to drive off, he turned back to us and said, "Ready?" We nodded. I asked how long it would take us and he said more than one hour.

As we piled out of the car and into the beautiful open-air lobby of the hotel, Wayan handed me his card, "Message for any tourist adventure. What day are you returning to the airport?" he asked. "Tomorrow or the next day," I said. We exchanged salutations and I took the card and nodded.

After a great night's sleep, I awoke to the site of the valley and the jungle below. I wanted to visit a local mosque and inquired at the front desk if they knew what time the prayers were and where there was a mosque. The concierge at the front desk called a Muslim colleague who offered that the Mushollah Ubudiyah was the closest place to pray, as all bigger mosques were on the other side of the island. He thought the adhan would be at 1 pm.

I sent Wayan a message, and a few hours later, he was back in his black SUV with a new batik shirt at the entrance of the hotel. We got in the car, and as he was pulling out of the steep driveway, he asked where we wanted to go. Monkey Forest, Wood Carving, Rice Paddies, Coffee? We both looked at each other. "Wayan can we start by going to the mosque?" I replied.

"Okay okay. Monkeys?" he asked inquisitively in response.

I realized that my use of the word mosque was not resonating with Wayan. "Masjid, can we go to the masjid for the adhan," I continued.

"Masjid?" He put his foot on the break and turned back to look at me. "Masjid?" he repeated again, seeming surprised.

"Yes," I said. "Masjid. Do you know where there is a masjid near to here?"

"Yes, I think there is one small one," he said, gesturing in the direction of the mosque.

"Okay great, let's go," I responded.

As we pulled out of the driveway onto the main road, Wayan looked back at us and said, "First you want to go to wood carving?"

"Can we first go to the masjid and then wood carving?" I said.

"Okay, Okay," he said.

"Do you know the way to Mushollah Ubudiyah?" I asked. Wayan lit up with recognition.

"Ubudiyah Masjid. You want to go to Ubudiyah?"

And we were off. I had, as I always do, attempted to calculate the prayer times for Ubud before making the plan to visit the mosque. I had searched for the prayer times on Islamic Prayer Finder and saw that the call was at 12:27 pm. I had asked Wayan to pick us up at 11:45 am and he was on time, maybe even early.

Wayan informed us that there is a big Muslim area in Bali, but not near to the hotel. He said that the area that is very Muslim has a big mosque if we wanted to go there, because Ubudiyah is a very small mosque. I said thank you and that for that day, we wanted to go to Ubudiyah.

It was clear that Wayan wasn't completely certain where the Ubudiyah mosque was, but he knew the road it was on. I watched our blue dot move on my Google Maps app and as we passed the point where Google thought the mosque was located, I said "Wayan I think it is there." Wayan made a big u-turn on a small but busy two-lane street. He stuck the nose of the car far into the lane of oncoming traffic, making all of the cars and motorbikes come to a halt. He pulled up toward a long skinny driveway and stopped the car while pointing to the narrow driveway. "Masjid," he said.

The driveway looked like a motorcycle parking lot. On the right, just past the motorbikes and before we entered the back area, there was a half wall with text carved into the stone that read, welcome to Ubudiyah Foundation Building. The sign didn't say anything about a mosque; however, the shiny black plaque below the text was adorned with an ornate Arabic script. There was a blue arrow on the sign pointing toward the building. A glance inward revealed a very dark interior walkway. At the end of the driveway was the front porch of someone's home. Wayan had adventured into the back where a man was eating his lunch, and had brought the man to speak with us. "Hello," I said. "We are looking for the masjid." "Yes," said the man. "It is just in there." The man pointed toward the dark walkway. Wayan looked at me and pointed toward the stoop of the house where the man had been eating his lunch, indicating he would wait there for us.

We walked into the dark passageway. There was no light in the walkway with the exception of a bright patch of sunlight streaming in from a hole in the wall, which revealed a fading green and white coat of paint. The passageway snaked into darkness, until finally I could see a few steps up ahead that led into light. We continued toward the steps, navigating over puddles of water, fallen broomsticks, and electrical wires. Once we emerged from the walkway, we were in a large open area with concrete flooring. The natural light was coming in through small windows somewhere up high, and everything felt calm and quiet. There was a bench in the large open area where one man sat. There was another man napping on the ground. I could see signs at the far end of the open area for women's and men's rooms, and a few other signs I could not make sense of. To the left, there was a large elevated prayer hall up five or six steps, in front of which there were many pairs of shoes. I gestured toward the man on the bench.

"Adhan? Adhan time?" I asked. Both the man who had been napping and the man on the bench looked at me, but it was clear they were not sure what to say. My mind leapt to whether or not we would be welcomed. I had been welcomed at every mosque I'd visited, but we were foreigners, inappropriately dressed, and very unannounced. I took off my sandals and walked toward the two men. Heidi looked at me and followed. Just then the man who had been eating his lunch outside emerged from the dark passageway and looked toward us. "The adhan is at 12:40 pm." I smiled and thanked him.

The man who had been resting on the floor stood up and he and the man on the bench both gestured toward us and then to the far side of the prayer area. "Ladies, ladies," they said. "Yes," I smiled. "We will go there." We walked to the far side, where there was a sign that read Wanita, meaning woman in Bahasa. I had noticed the same sign on the women's bathroom at the airport. The sign was accompanied by a monochromatic image of a head with arms, legs, and a triangle at the bottom. The ubiquitous female symbol. Behind the Wanita sign was a spigot for wudu, or ablution, the ritual washing before prayer. We were not going to pray so we did not perform wudu. Instead, we turned around to head up the stairs to the prayer room.

We were both wearing shorts and short sleeve shirts, a disrespectful and inappropriate way to enter a mosque. I couldn't believe our clothing had slipped my mind as I was usually very cognizant of such details, especially after living in the U.A.E. for six years where modest dress was expected in public. I could not believe that I had forgotten to bring a headscarf from the hotel, an item that has been on my packing list for every trip for years.

The prayer area, a large rectangle, took up most of the interior space of the building. At the front of the rectangle was a concrete archway, what I assumed was the mihrab, a space that faced the direction of Mecca, and inside of it a wooden podium and microphone. At the top of the mihrab was an LED panel that had scrolling information, starting with the five daily prayers and the times they would sound. I waited for the clock to reach the Dhuhr, and it said Dhuhr -12:27. There were three rows of green carpet runners laid out in front of the mihrab, with lines on them, and there were assorted bookshelves with Qur'an in them. There were only four men up front near the mihrab, a few in pants and a few in sarongs, traditional Indonesian attire. Beyond the rows of prayer carpets, there was a large empty green tiled floor. Up and down the space, there were pillars holding up the ceiling, which was painted a light blue and inlaid with a decorative coffering in white. There were metal rods running horizontally across the midway point of the pillars, from which green curtains hung. The fabric gathered and draped over the top of the rods, like a shower curtain on cleaning days (figure 12.1 and recording 15).

A man walked towards us and dropped the green curtain, creating an enclosed square area on the ladies' side of the prayer hall. He gestured for us to come to the area, but both Heidi and I were hesitant, because of our inappropriate clothing. He began speaking with someone behind us in Bahasa, and all I could understand was sarong. I looked over my shoulder, and it was Wayan. They were discussing the need for us to wear sarongs. The man walked into the green-curtained area he had just created and grabbed something from the shelf and gestured toward us. It looked like he was holding a piece of black fabric.

Wayan looked at us and said sarong, while gesturing the act of wrapping something around his waist. The man put the black fabric back on the shelf and walked back toward the front of the prayer room. Heidi and I again

Figure 12.1 Ubudiyah Foundation Building Mushollah, Bali, Indonesia.

Bali, Indonesia, 2017

Recording #15   Ubudiyah Foundation Building Mushollah, Bali, Indonesia—Dhuhr Adhan.

looked at each other. I walked up the stairs quickly into the curtained-off area. I was familiar with religious spaces that were separated by curtains mostly in the context of Orthodox Jewish temples, and Emirati weddings. While we could see some of the men through the gaps between the curtain and the poles, it felt very private inside the enclosed curtained space. I walked over to the shelf, where the man had put back the fabrics, and saw that there was an entire collection of abayas for women to place over their clothes. I felt so anxious and out of place about us both wearing shorts, that I opened the first one I could get my hands on and placed it over my head and wiggled into the covering. There was an elastic band along the hole for my head, which I placed on top of my head like a headband, and two very tiny holes for the hands. All three holes were tight around. I handed Heidi a black one, but when she put it on it was only a top. I looked back at the shelf and noticed a piece of fabric with a matching print and handed that to her as well, it was the accompanying bottom. We looked at each other and smiled.

   I grabbed my audio recorder. I took the recorder out of my bag, but before I could turn it on, the same man who had dropped the curtain and offered us the garments was reciting the adhan. I turned my phone on and fumbled to turn on the recorder, then stood very still. Halfway through the recitation, the green curtain opened, and a girl in a school uniform walked in. She didn't look like she was more than fourteen years old. Her school uniform was a skirt and short-sleeve shirt. She went toward the cabinet of garments and picked one up and placed it over her school uniform, just as we had done with ours. She then placed the elastic band around the back of her head, so I discreetly moved my strap into the proper position. I imagined that the girl must have seen both of us, and me with the elastic strap on top of my head, and thought to herself, what is going on here. The adhan concluded. I exhaled.

   I looked up at the LED panel, which now said IQM: -5 Minutes. The scrolling clock was saying that the iqamah, the second call to prayer or the final recitation before the prayer, would begin in five minutes. The iqamah, I have learned, is the recitation made moments before the prayer begins, and it is often recited very quickly and in more of a spoken than melodic voicing by the muezzin or imam. The iqamah uses one of each of the repeated verses of the adhan, and then before the final "Allahu akbar, Allahu akbar," there is a phrase not in the adhan. This line, "Qad qamati-ssalah, qad qamati-ssalah," roughly translates to, "prayer is to begin, prayer is to begin." The imam leads the prayer directly after the iqamah is recited.

I decided I would record the iqamah as well. I took my audio recorder and phone and placed them toward the side of the prayer cube. The schoolgirl was now prostrating in prayer. So as not to not disturb her, I moved to the back of the space. The iqamah was recited and then the prayers began. I successfully recorded the iqamah. Heidi and I looked at one another and decided it was time for us to leave. With some difficulty, we removed our outer garments and placed them back on the shelf. I grabbed my bag and we slipped out of the curtained area and down the stairs. I turned around to look back toward the prayer area and there were now a dozen men gathered in prayer. Heidi and I took in the space for a minute, before proceeding to the shoe area and then back out the dark hallway toward the driveway. We emerged from the dark walkway and saw Wayan sitting on the step, having some lunch. We took a walk and discussed the experience in the mushollah, and when he was finished eating, we all jumped into the car to head off to the wood-carving factory.

When we arrived at the wood-carving factory, we met Suardika, a saleswoman for the factory who explained the process and materials to us, took us through the steps that the artisans went through when carving the wood, and guided us through the showroom of beautiful, ornately carved wooden statues and sculptures. Many of the pieces were of Hindu Gods, not surprisingly, given that Bali is a predominantly Hindu-populated island of Indonesia. Indonesia is a majority Muslim country and has the largest Muslim population of any country in the world, hovering around 225 million. After we had browsed the collection for a while on our own, Suardika found us and took us back through certain areas, offering us large discounts.

> "I will give you the friends' discount, she said. I will give you 50% off anything."

This was a great discount; however, the items were expensive. She then accompanied us through the store and took it upon herself to describe many of the statues and designs. In an effort to learn more about Bali, I asked Suardika how the economy was doing. She said it was strong; however, the recent volcanic eruptions meant many tourists were afraid to visit the island and so tourism was lower than usual.

> But, there is plenty of food for everyone, she went on. Also, here in Bali we pray a lot, we take a lot of our money for prayer and everyone, all the people, pray

a lot. It is for this reason that we have had no damage and no problems. Yes, the volcano erupted but no people were hurt, it is very safe here and the tourists should not be scared." I nodded my head and listened. "Even the tsunami, do you remember the tsunami?" she asked. I assumed she meant the tsunami of 2005, which I did of course remember. "In Java the tsunami hit very hard, but here in Bali, we had no problems, even until now no problems, because we are all good people here, we are Hindus and Hindus pray and pray and so we are protected. We are many good people here. How do you find the Balinese people?" she asked.

"Very nice," I said, "everyone has been very nice."

"Yes, see that is what, the people here-everyone is working, and eating well, and the economy is good, and also giving money and food for prayer, and all people are praying, and because of this it is very safe and good here."

I nodded my head. I understood what she was saying, and it sat a little uneasy with me. "So Bali is mostly Hindu?" I asked.

"Yes, yes Bali is Hindu," Suardika replied.

"And Indonesia is mostly a Muslim country, isn't that so?" I asked.

"Yes, there are many Hindus here in Bali, but also there are Muslims and Christians and Buddhists. All the people live here in Bali in peace. You know here the Hindus are welcoming and friends with everyone, Muslim or Buddhist it doesn't matter, all are friends. But in Java, I would not go to live in Java, because as a Hindu, I would not be welcome there, the people are not so friendly," she concluded.

Chapter 13

Sound as Memory

The relationship between sound and memory has been explored and researched by scientists and scholars alike. Beyond the basic memory recall that listening to a recording affords us—recalling who or what was recorded—I have found that listening back to field recordings evokes a deeper bodily memory of each encounter. The type and extent of the bodily responses to these sounds vary depending on the events that took place while making the recording. Through the process of listening back to field recordings on the soundmap for the purposes of writing this book, I was surprised by the information and memory recall I experienced. I, of course, better remembered events of a day that occurred two years ago after listening to a recording from that day, but also experienced bodily responses when listening, ranging from getting chills in my legs and the hairs on my arm standing up, to reexperiencing emotions I felt the day I recorded. This was surprising to me. Through listening back to hundreds of recordings, I found a unifying factor in my bodily memory experiences: nonlinguistic sounds evoked a bodily response more frequently, compared to sounds involving language.

Sound studies scholars and composers have over the years developed language and taxonomies for differentiating the ways people listen. These correlate an approach to listening with the process our brains use to make sense of vibration and sound. Pierre Schaeffer was a radio engineer and announcer who was fascinated by the way recording and broadcasting changed how people could hear and listen to sound. His thinking was influenced by philosopher Edmund Husserl, founder of phenomenology, and in 1966, Schaeffer wrote *Traité des Objects Musicaux*,[1] his attempt at an analytical theory for sound-based work. Within this work, Schaeffer articulates the four functions of listening. This includes Listening [Écouter]—the recognition or identification of the event that produced a given sound; Perceiving [Ouïr]—receiving the sound for the sound itself without looking for meaning in or interpreting the sound; Hearing [Entendre]—recognizing the properties of a sound; and Comprehending [Comprendre]—the understanding of a message that is communicated or transmitted by sound.[2]

Inspired by Schaeffer's functions of listening and informed by new research in audition, in 1994, Michel Chion offered the three modes of listening. These are causal listening, "listening to a sound in order to gather information about its cause (or source)"[3]; semantic listening, "that which refers to a code or a language to interpret a message"[4]; and reduced listening, originally named by Schaeffer to refer to "the listening mode that focuses on the traits of the sound itself."[5] Schaeffer and Chion created sound classifications that rely on the way our brains interpret or make sense of sounds our ears hear. Schaeffer seemed most concerned with distinguishing between direct listening, where sound sources are visible, and acousmatic listening where the sound source or cause is hidden.[6] These listening modes are tied to how people understand and make sense of sounds based on how well they can understand their origin or meaning. I think it may be time to consider modes of listening that differentiate between how our body hears, specifically that which our brains process and that which is processed by the rest of our bodies. Our bodies are also involved in taking in sonic information and I have come to believe that when we listen but are not focused on making meaning from sound, similar to reduced listening, our bodies are more present in the listening process. This is very similar to how I was listening on the rooftop in Rajasthan, where the wedding sounds were consuming me, forming shapes in my mind and circling about in my awareness, even though I was not listening for meaning. In other words, we use more of our body than simply our ears and brain to take in sound.

The field recordings on the soundmap capture the call to prayer, along with large amounts of supplementary sound data, sounds that were not the focus of the recording but which were included in it anyway. This data, the bulk of which was recorded before and sometimes after the adhan is recited, includes a wide range of environmental and human sounds like the footsteps of passersby, the closing and opening of doors, the zooming of cars, distortion of recorded sound due to wind or amplification, and other prominent but distant sounds like airplanes, church bells, and other adhan. This supplementary sound information serves as a sonic journal and has proven useful in helping to situate my memory back at the place and time when a recording was made. The primary sonic information in the recordings, the adhan itself and sometimes conversations with others, helps me recall the chronology of the visit, the details of exchanges with community members, and nuances about the sounding or recitation of the call to prayer.

I have found the supplementary sound data to work very differently on my memory. It seems that these sounds I did not intend to record, but which I heard through my headphones while monitoring the recording, jump-start my recollection of other, sense-based memories from the day of the recording. This has included remembering some of the feelings I had on that day, and triggering a deeper connection to the encounter, which allows me to more fully recall details that are not captured in the recording. These moments of sonic memory recall can often be triggered by listening to just a few minutes of a recording of supplementary sounds, and the result might be recalling hours of that same day not included in the recording.

In trying to understand more about the sound/body memory connection, I turned to J. Martin Daughtry's *Listening to War: Sound, Music, Trauma, and Survival in Wartime Iraq*. In his book, Daughtry explores the relationship between sound and trauma, by considering how "listening to" or "listening for" sound can serve as a trigger for bodily memories connected to the environment and experiences in which those sounds were heard.[7] Daughtry's research is focused on wartime sounds in Iraq, and is based on the testimonials of Iraqi civilians and American service members. He notes that for "people living in combat zones, sounds command extreme attention."[8] For Daughtry, this notion is tied to the way audition becomes a form of survival, as people learn how to filter out sounds of danger from ordinary sounds, and how this hyper-focus can contribute to sound being a trauma trigger. While the trauma responses Daughtry speaks of are tied to war-zone sonic triggers and heightened emotional states including fear and anxiety, which are not as salient to the research in this book, his research on the connection between certain sounds one focuses on and a person's bodily response to rehearing the same or similar sounds is well-documented and compelling. For this reason, I find this connection of hyper-focus on sound and its ability to trigger a bodily response to be a good starting point for unpacking bodily memory that a field recordist may experience with their own field recordings.

The process of recording, when done well, requires hyper-focus on an environment, similar to the type that Daughtry writes about. When I record, I am fiercely focused on my surroundings, taking everything in, understanding where generators may be placed, where traffic is loudest, and hearing the environment in a way I ordinarily would not in my daily life. I am completely focused on what I am hearing in the environment around me. Once I place headphones on to monitor my field recorder, I am then immersed in that same sonic environment in a more all-encompassing way. My headphones create sonic isolation between the sounds of the world around me and the amplified way I hear those sounds through the microphones and pre-amplifiers in my audio recorder. To turn up the volume and detail of this sonic environment, I simply need to adjust a dial, and suddenly a bird chirping ten feet away feels as though it is right next to me. I don't understand the details of how the ear and the brain store this sonic information as memory, or why deeper focus may contribute to deeper recall. However, listening back to the field recordings I made while hyper-focused on the sounds triggers a bodily memory in response to the sounds I hear. These bodily responses often help me recall greater detail about the encounter than what is contained in the recording itself. This is to say my body seems to store the memories each time I record, and relistening to a field recording, which I recorded while listening with great focus and attention, brings my body and mind back to the moment when the recording was made, allowing me to recall the event in great detail beyond that which is captured in the recording.

Having worked on this project for more than ten years now, there are many recordings made at many mosques, the memories of which can easily blend together or be largely forgotten. Listening to field recordings helps me place myself in a given mosque, on a particular street, or in conversation with community members I have not thought about for years. Sound is a more powerful tool for memory recall than my written notes of a visit, or even photographs taken at a mosque. While listening back to field recordings of the adhan, sounds of gates creaking or cars passing before, during, or after the adhan can profoundly impact my recollection of that day. The sonic environment revealed through the recordings not only helps to situate my memory back in the physical environment I was in when recording, but also helps with recall of people, objects, happenings, exchanges, and feelings that occurred during a visit which I might have otherwise forgotten. In some instances, listening to field recordings has reminded me of the anxiety I felt on the day of recording, events that occurred earlier the same day that are unrelated, the feeling of the wind's chill on my skin, the nuisance and itchiness of mosquito bites on my ankles, and so on. Often, small sonic details can unlock a chain of body-based memories from the day I recorded, even when this day was years ago. These sonically-induced bodily memories and responses feed directly into my writing of the case studies in this book and contribute to the depth of detail that I am able to include.

In 2012, I spent a week traveling and recording the call to prayer in Jordan. I brought with me a Sound Devices 702T recorder with a shotgun microphone and a stereo capsule microphone, all packed neatly in a bright orange pelican case. I rented a car with my girlfriend, and we traveled around the country, stopping at nearby mosques as prayer time approached. One day, I was attempting to record the Dhuhr around mid-day at a small neighborhood mosque off of a main road that connected Amman to Aqaba.

We drove up alongside the mosque fifteen minutes before prayer time, and I began assembling my equipment and running a sound check. Before I had finished, the car was surrounded by children, all of whom had at least one question for me. They wanted to talk, they wanted to see the equipment, and

Figure 13.1 Masjid Talha bin Obaidullah, Al-Ain Al-Baida, Jordan.

because there were seven to ten of them, they made a lot of noise. You can imagine the challenge of trying to record the adhan in that context, where "Hello, hello, what is your name?" obscures the sound of the call. When I listen back to the recording from this day, I can recall my novice-ness to field recording at mosques, and I can hear my hesitance about how to talk to the children who were Arabic-speaking, my fear that an adult from the community might approach me or be unhappy that I chose to stop in their village, and my hyper-focus on the mission of recording the adhan. I did show the children the equipment and let them listen through the headphones as my recorder was capturing our exchanges.

When the adhan was about to sound, I looked at the children and placed my finger over my closed lips and gave them a look with very big eyes. They all

Recording #16 Masjid Talha bin Obaidullah, Al-Ain Al-Baida, Jordan.

looked at one another and placed their fingers over their lips. The recording of the adhan from that day is not punctuated by the voices of children asking me my name, though you can still hear them whispering in the background. Each time I listen to the unedited field recording from this day, the children's voices surrounding me through the stereo capsule microphone remind me of this memory and the details of my trip to Dana Castle in Jordan (figure 13.1 and recording 16).

Chapter 14

Al Dabb'iya, United Arab Emirates, 2014

There was a green garden at the front of the mosque, with grass and shrubs that added a splash of color to the otherwise beige and dust scene surrounding the empty lot. The warm air rushed in as I opened the passenger door of Anna's black Jeep Cherokee. It was late May of 2014 and the weather had already turned toward warm but wasn't yet the oppressive 110–120 degrees Fahrenheit that came in the heart of the summer months. The dust was brought to life by a teenage boy in a crisp white kandura, zipping around the sidewalks and through the mega bazaar parking area, kicking up dust in the wake of what looked like a cross between a self-built soapbox and a low to the ground dune buggy. It was bright red under a thick coat of dust with small fat black tires, and was louder as the boy accelerated, louder than a motorcycle.

Anna and I often went on adventures together. She was my Abu Dhabi adventure buddy. The adventures included raiding trash rooms for parts to make decorative lamps, excursions to camel beauty pageants, and haggling with the caretakers of dilapidated buildings marked for demolition in order to purchase secondhand items that remained behind in the old apartments—the closest we could get to a garage sale in Abu Dhabi. One Saturday, Anna asked if I would be interested in venturing out to Al Dabb'iya with her as she wanted to see the beautiful seaside. Al Dabb'iya is a forty-five-minute drive outside of Abu Dhabi City in a westerly direction along a narrow two-lane road called the Abu Dhabi-Ghweifat International Highway. The highway travels just inland along the coast of the Strait of Hormuz, toward and away from the UAE's border with Saudi Arabia.

I packed my audio recording equipment and a bottle of water before heading downstairs, where I waited in the air-conditioned lobby for Anna's car to pull up. Anna wisely purchased a car when she first arrived in Abu Dhabi, a commitment I couldn't wrap my head around having moved so far from

Chapter 14

home, and constantly anticipating my return there. She bought a four-wheel drive Jeep Cherokee that was good for commuting as well as desert camping and dune bashing. We were camping buddies and I had experienced the joys of driving her car on the dunes with deflated tires, feeling my stomach drop as I would fly over a crest and the car would fishtail its way to its footing. The Jeep came into view.

The lobby's automatic glass doors opened. I walked out toward Anna's car. Its black facade was always covered in a thin layer of Abu Dhabi dust, the name I affectionately give to the tiny sand particles that fly through the air unnoticed until they settle creating a thin coating on everything. I opened the back door, threw my gear in and climbed upfront.

"Hi there, how's it going?"

"Hi there, thanks for coming on this adventure with me," Anna remarked in a funny little kid voice, before throwing the car into drive and circling around the building toward the exit.

"You are going to navigate, okay?"

"Yup, sounds good. How do you spell Dabb'iya?" I asked.

"Dabbaiya, I think. Just look it up on the map. It is west of Abu Dhabi on one of the small land masses jutting out."

"Okay I think I found it. You want to drive all the way down Airport Road, and we can take it from there," I directed.

Anna's car, Yeep bin Anna Al Dechert, a name conjured from hilarious mispronunciations of Jeep paired with an Arabification of Anna's name, delineates the Jeep as her son in traditional Emirati naming convention. Yeep takes her to and from work, out to happy hours, dinners, desert camping, and on adventures such as ours. It also has a few creeks, aches, and pains, including electric windows that occasionally fail when they are already halfway open, and my least favorite quirk, a 120 kilometer per hour indicator, that beeps very loudly whenever the car is driven over 120 km/h. Unlike many cars with similar warnings that alert you to your "overspeeding," as it is referred to in the Emirates, then switch off, Yeep bin Anna Al Dechert just keeps beeping for as long as you are driving over the speed limit. You might imagine that this proves particularly annoying when driving on highways, many of which have speed limits that are 140 km/h. To compensate for this annoying beeping, car rides with Anna entail very loud and often bad radio music that blasts along the highway portions of the ride to keep all inside the car from going mad.

The narrow Ghweifat Highway is packed with trucks, some petrol tankers, and many semis carrying construction materials, making the drive particularly un-scenic. As we neared where I thought the Al Dabb'iya exit would be, Anna moved toward the right lane to exit. Unfortunately, the dust being kicked up by the truck in front of us made it impossible to see the small exit sign and we missed the turn. We found a turnaround point not too far up the road, and made our way back.

Al Dabb'iya is a small sleepy seaside town, located near to a large oil rig. As we turned off the exit road, we could see the oil rig compound on our left side through huge metal gates, separating us from what was going on inside. We drove past the gate, and a little way down the road we came upon a housing community. I knew little about the place, except that it had a history of being inhabited by some Bedouin families during pearl diving season. I had met an Emirati woman while working with a local heritage project, who told me that her family still traveled to Dabb'iya and had built a house there where they all went for weekend getaways.

We entered the area with all of the houses and traveled down what looked like newly paved roads that were pristine and without a skid mark on them. They were covered in a thin layer of dust and surrounded by newly built homes, all a light beigey peach color. On the left-hand side, we saw a paved rectangular parking area slightly elevated on a hill next to the water.

"This must be where my friends camped," Anna remarked. "It isn't all that impressive, but the water is beautiful."

It's important to note that camping in the UAE is often accompanied by stunning surroundings, whether they be rocky mountain terrain, dried-up wadis, or my personal favorite, the red sand dunes of the Rub al Khali desert. We strolled around the patch of asphalt, gazing out at the water before getting back into Yeep and continuing on.

We drove a loop around the main road to get a sense of the place. All of the homes were facing the water, many with large fences around them common in the UAE, and large wooden dhows in the driveways. We came upon a few unfinished or half-paved roads where a stop sign had been placed, after which there was just dirt and sand, no more road. The road to nowhere was not a completely unfamiliar concept to me. From my apartment window in Abu Dhabi I could see several unfinished roads to nowhere as part of new construction projects. I always wondered if perhaps the other half of these roads, the part that happens after the stop sign, were deemed unnecessary or were part of a future phase of the project. It makes you wonder, if they never finish the road, as was the case with the road to nowhere in Al Dabb'iya, do they take the stop sign down?

Slightly further up the road, we passed a small convenience store, Al Dabeeiyya Grocery, which sold cigarettes, chips, and sodas, the type of shop we call a bodega in New York City, or a Baqala in Abu Dhabi City. Just beyond the grocery was the Sheikh Mubarak bin Mohammed Mosque, a beautiful large Moroccan-style mosque that seemed to be the centerpiece of Al Dabb'iya. Anna pulled Yeep into the parking lot, and as we opened the doors, the air was filled with a zooming noise. I instinctually turned to look in the direction the sound was coming from, and saw the teenage boy in the crisp white kandura riding around in his small red vehicle. He was flying around the parking lot, jumping curbs and leaving large dust plumes in his wake. I got lost in listening to the vroom vrooming, moving toward and away from us, and in watching the zig-zagging path of the car and accompanying clouds of dust.

I turned my gaze in the opposite direction so that I was facing the mosque. Realizing some time had passed, I glanced at my phone for the time. I grabbed the orange pelican case and moved it to the edge of the backseat, popped open the latches, and began to assemble my equipment. Inside, I had packed a Sound Devices 702T recorder and an Audio Technica stereo capsule microphone. I placed the windscreen over the microphone, plugged the two XLR cables in and powered up the recorder. While placing the large sound-isolating headphones over my ears, I fiddled with the microphone-input-level adjustments and headphone-level adjustments, so as to not blow out my hearing. The zooming car continued to be prominently featured in the soundscape, and I began monitoring the sounds of the environment. I telescoped the boom pole out a few feet and gently twisted it to point the microphone in a variety of directions to get a sense of the movement of the wind, the best way to use Yeep to block out the zooming noise near the grocery, and of course to try and find a suitable level for recording the adhan. Anna was standing at the end of the boom pole as I hovered over the knobs on the audio recorder, my head inside the car. "Hello, can you hear me?" Anna whispered into the microphone, her lips touching the windscreen.

I turned and looked her right in the eyes. I could hear her like she was whispering directly in my ear. She smiled at me with her eyes, then whispered, "cheese balls," as a grin formed on her face. I threw her a dirty look and moved the microphone away from her head and redirected it toward the mosque. I pressed record.

No cars had pulled into the parking lot, as was usual around prayer time, nor had anyone walked up to the mosque and set their sandals aside at the door to enter and pray. I took off my headphones and approached the only person I saw, a man who was walking through the creaky metal gate into the mosque garden. "Excuse me, what time is the adhan?" I asked. He didn't respond, continuing to tend to the plants in front of him. I wondered if perhaps he didn't hear me, or we didn't speak the same language. Maybe an unfamiliar woman speaking to him made him uncomfortable. I looked at Anna and said, "Well maybe the mosque isn't open yet," implying that just as we were in a town with roads to nowhere, perhaps this was a not yet active mosque.

I put my headphones back on. The sonic environment inside my headphones always feels like a secret world that others can't hear. I could hear the flies buzzing around the microphone so clearly as though each flap of their wings was isolated and present. The birds were chirping from different directions, making my head involuntarily turn as they approached. The metal gate through which the man who was gardening walked created a loud squeak every time it was opened or closed. And in the background was the vroom vroom and audible dust plumes of the teenage boy in his crisp kandura. Then I heard it, the sound of the amplification system switching on. I listen closely for this sound whenever I am trying to record the adhan. Over time, I have learned that this is often the sound of the switch on the muezzin's microphone being flipped from the off position to the on position. Shortly after the sound of the switch flipping, the adhan would begin. I placed my hand on the level knob for the microphones.

"Allahu Akbar, Allahu Akbar."

The adhan began. I adjusted the levels just slightly after the first line, not wanting to change the level in the middle of a line of recitation, as this would be tricky to fix in post. Anna had also stopped whatever else she had been doing, and we both just listened. I kept my hand on the microphone gain knob, my eyes glued to the decibel meter to make sure that the recording did not clip. After the second verse, I relaxed and took in the visual environment

Recording #17 Sheikh Mubarak bin Mohammed Mosque, Al Dabb'iya, United Arab Emirates—Asr Adhan.

of the mosque as it paired with the secret sound world in my headphones. The vrooming sounds had faded into the distance as the muezzin's beautiful voice filled the space. The birds continued to chirp, and the squeaky gate continued to squeak. The adhan concluded. No one appeared to pray, and the sleepy town was still sleepy. Anna and I took one final look around, then hopped into Yeep and drove off back toward the city (recording 17).

Chapter 15

Copenhagen, Denmark, 2017

PART I: 9/11

Buckland 208 was my first dorm room at Mount Holyoke College. I moved into the room in early September 2000. By the time I showed up to move in, my first year roommate's side of the room had already been done up with a larger-than-life Derek Jeter poster above the bed. I adorned my side of the wall with photos of family and artwork, blue-tacked up above my bed framing the blue comforter. We were great at sharing, co-existing, and even throwing parties for the floor. Two floors up, in Buckland 408, were two other first years, let's call them Kasey and Nikki. Kasey was a granola girl from Vermont who loved reggae, had taken a gap year on Rotary in Thailand and had big hair, while Nikki was an equestrian who had questionable taste in boyfriends and a zebra blanket on her bed. While we didn't exactly share a ceiling and a floor, we became friends. Kasey and I hit it off right away in that we shared a passion for photography, travel, and adventure. We would spend our time talking about how amazing it would be to take a trip to somewhere on the African continent or India. Our friendship grew through shared academic interests, and we found ourselves taking the local bus to class at the University of Massachusetts once a week for darkroom photography and later for an Anthropology course. It shouldn't be a surprise that after college, our paths continued to twist and turn toward and then away from one another throughout the phases of our life.

Shortly after college, Kasey pursued a fellowship in India. She was living in Jaipur when I took a three-month trip to visit a college friend in Delhi. Jaipur and Delhi are a five-hour bus ride apart from one another, very close by Indian travel standards. Kasey and I met up several times during that three months. Based on her recommendation and my desire to spend more time in India, I decided to apply for the same fellowship, which I was awarded the following year. After our time in India, our paths turned away from each other for a while as Kasey moved to Dhaka, Bangladesh, and I moved to Abu Dhabi, UAE. One day out of the blue, I got an email from Kasey asking about what it was like living in Abu Dhabi, as she was considering a job there. Within a few days, she had accepted an offer, and just like that our paths crossed again. This time, as serendipity would have it, her school moved her into the Twinkle building, affectionately named after the huge neon sign that hung from the front, adorned with several stars that advertised the ladies-only nail salon on the fifth floor, ten steps from the front door of my building. Kasey and I were again in close proximity to one another, just like our first year in Buckland Hall at Mount Holyoke. We traveled to the Andaman Islands, celebrated American holidays together, and on occasion would meet up for a drink after a long week, or have a dinner and movie night at her place.

College was memorable for many reasons, not the least of which being the morning two planes crashed into the side of the World Trade Center buildings in downtown Manhattan. I had moved out of Buckland Hall by 2001 but returned often for meals. On the morning of 9/11, I had an early squash class that I was most likely late to, and was therefore running across campus. I have never been an early morning person, and the Kendall Sports Center was literally on the opposite side of campus from my dorm. When I arrived at class, huffing and puffing, I took a seat on the benches just outside the squash courts, as we all did at the beginning of each class. My heart was pounding hard from the mad dash to class to avoid getting a third late, which would translate to an absence, one more of which meant I would not get credit for the class.

At first, I didn't notice that anything was off, and since I had literally woken up, jumped out of bed, threw on clothes, and run across the campus, I hadn't any idea that this morning was different from any other. Remember these were pre-cell phone days for most college students. The teacher was rolling a television AV cart toward the benches where we sat. I thought, yes! Maybe we will watch a long video on squash technique, which would limit the amount of time we were on the courts. The cart was in place and plugged in, and the squash coach began to speak. Her tone was not as go-team-aggressive as usual. "Good morning," she began. "As some of you may know, something terrible has happened this morning." I remember feeling myself slowly coming back to the surface out of my own head and racing heartbeat, beginning to focus on the here and now as she spoke.

"In light of these events, school will be cancelled today. Televisions like this one will be on throughout the campus tuned to the news, and there will be counselors available for students to speak with." She paused and looked up at the big cathode-ray tube television box, strapped to the top shelf of the metal cart with a black nylon strap with teeth, a smaller version of what the tractor-trailers use to tie things safely to their flatbeds. The shelf below had a black VCR/DVD combo player, and next to it two remote controls velcroed to the cart so as not to be lost, each branded with a white label with black letters that said, television and VCR/DVD, respectively. The bottom of the cart held a power strip, where the plugs of each device terminated, and on the side of the cart were two protruding prongs, around which the length of the power cable could be wrapped for storage and easy rolling.

"You are welcome to stay here for the duration of the class and watch the news, but class is cancelled so you are also free to go," she concluded.

I looked around at the other students and then back up at the television where my gaze had been glued for a few minutes. I was staring at the television trying to make sense of it, I could see the two buildings, one with smoke billowing out from its side. I am from New York, so I knew I was looking at the World Trade Center, but my brain did not compute the information. The ticker on the bottom of the television read, airplane has flown into World Trade Center Tower in Manhattan. I still had no real sense of what was going on. But I was shy to admit that I was confused, so instead of asking the teacher or anyone else, I simply grabbed my things and made the long hike back to the opposite side of the campus. I reached the Buckland common room, a small living room on the ground floor where thirty students were huddled around the television, some crying, others holding their friends in their arms. I walked in and took a seat on the carpet facing the television and listened to what people were saying. Someone mentioned they were from New York, and that they had not gotten in touch with their family, another woman reacted by crying and running out of the room. I had wondered if people were dying. I realized then that I did not have a grasp of what was happening or the severity of the situation. It is strange how things can knock us out of our own lanes. We are moving forward in our own car, thinking about our own lives and then suddenly whack! There is an explosion or a crash or an event that requires us to be present beyond the walls of our car.[1]

It suddenly hit me, I was from New York. I hadn't even thought about calling my family and friends. I calmly and somewhat reluctantly left the crowd in the living room and returned to the emptiness of my dorm room. I sat alone, with my room phone next to me, trying to call friends and family. My father worked in the city and my best friend lived uptown. I had been able to reach my mom and Long Island family, and all were safe. My dad, on the other hand, was unreachable for a few days. As it turned out, he was safe but unable to get home because of the closure of all bridges, tunnels, and public transportation. He ended up sleeping in his Brooklyn office and walking home over a bridge to Long Island the following day. My friend was also fine, but cellular lines and pagers (yes there were pagers then) were all unreachable, or jammed, making it impossible to reach anyone on a cellular network for a few days.

PART II: COPENHAGEN

After three years of living and working in Abu Dhabi, Kasey took a new job in Copenhagen teaching at an international school there. That same year, I moved back to the United States after six years of living in Abu Dhabi. I returned to New York City, where I took a job working for a tech startup which had recently gone public. I hated the job and missed the Middle East. I tried hard to fit back into New York living, but as a mid-thirty-year-old working in tech, I first had to play quick catch up on learning about millennial culture, something I had no awareness of before my departure to the Middle East.

Kasey encouraged me to visit her in Copenhagen, where I had never been. As I already had plans to be in Sweden for a conference, I simply arranged to take a train to Copenhagen where I would spend a week with Kasey, exploring the city, catching up on life, and meeting her new boyfriend. I arrived on a Friday night around 6:30 pm. It was early December, and the winter markets and Danish holiday spirit were in full force. Kasey picked me up from the train and we headed back to her fifth-floor walkup. Kasey's Copenhagen apartment, while slightly different from her Abu Dhabi apartment, maintained a similar energy and ambiance. The pink couch she'd had made by a Bangladeshi carpenter in Dhaka, which had dominated her Abu Dhabi living room, wouldn't fit up the stairwell of the Copenhagen building, so a black leather couch took its place. And the large low square coffee table, which had been painted pastel green and had doubled as a dining room table in Abu Dhabi, was now painted white and used as a coffee table for the new black couch.

Kasey had quickly adopted the Danish approach to transportation and already had two bicycles, her new speedy red one, and the old solid black one. We dropped my bags off in the apartment and within ten minutes were on the bicycles in the dark, biking to a Vietnamese restaurant in the downtown for dinner. I loved biking in Copenhagen. It took me a while to get used to the black bicycle, which was stuck in third gear and had a large basket in front, but once I got the hang of it, getting anywhere in Copenhagen was easy. Following behind Kasey and learning how the bike lanes worked were key to my success.

I had, prior to arriving, floated the idea of going to a local mosque together to record the call to prayer. Kasey seemed game for the idea, and we decided to go Sunday late morning to catch the adhan at the Imam Ali Moskeen in

Nørrebro, a twenty-minute bike ride away. Most of my friends have never been inside a mosque, and while I don't often take people with me when I record, I sometimes do and always enjoy sharing the process with others. When with someone else, I become acutely aware of my process, and the considerations that go into a visit to a mosque.

I grabbed my audio recorder and a hat, along with my warm clothes, scarf, and gloves, and we jumped on the bikes. Kasey navigated for us, and we traveled to a new part of town I had not yet been. It was clear as we got closer to the mosque that Copenhagen had a distinctly Muslim part of the city which we were traveling through. Not only was it evident in the clothing worn by people walking down the street—we did see more women wearing hijabs and men with beards and in kurta pajamas—but it was also obvious by the number of shawarma shops and kebab houses and by the Muslim household names that were connected to everyday shops, like Al Zhara Grocery. The writing on shop signs and store windows was now in Arabic and Danish, and there were many halal restaurants and clothing stores that sold hijabs and abayas.

We took our final turn off of the main road, Frederikssundsvej, at a halal restaurant called Medina. I looked down at my phone and saw that it was five minutes to the adhan. We peddled a block and a half off the main road, and just beyond the school playground was a stunningly gorgeous Iranian-style mosque with two tall turquoise minarets reaching up to the sky. There were three men gathered around the open hood of a car just outside the mosque. We peddled up and I asked what time the adhan was. One man with a beard told me, it would just be in a few minutes. I thanked him and we peddled our bicycles across the street and on to the sidewalk where we locked them. I grabbed my recorder out of the bike basket, and Kasey and I walked toward the mosque. The gentleman with the beard looked at us and said ladies' entrance, and pointed in the direction of a door at the end of the pathway. "Shukran," I responded. I had never been inside an Iranian mosque before, but was familiar with the distinctive and beautiful turquoise design.

Kasey had her large woolen scarf over her hair, and I had my hat on. We opened the door to the ladies' entrance and walked inside. There was a shoe rack in front of us, and we both removed our shoes, after which we walked up the staircase to the ladies' prayer room. The prayer room was flooded with natural light that streamed through large windows, which took up the entire back wall of the room. The floor was covered with beautifully woven and overlapping Iranian carpets. I had seen this carpet design many times before, when I would visit Mohammed at the carpet shop around the corner from my apartment in Abu Dhabi. I would spend hours in his shop each week, walking on and learning about carpet designs, materials, and their origins. The carpets in the ladies' prayer room were silk carpets with beautiful soft colors, representative of a more modern weaving style. The design was what I had always called a spider web. The pattern originates at the center of the carpet and moves outward with a thick blue web-like pattern of interconnected diamonds. The trim of the carpets was a royal blue, which created a warm contrast with the silky white tassels that hung over the edges. The carpets, of which there were probably twenty, seemed to be designed as companion pieces, most likely commissioned for the mosque.

Unlike many other ladies' prayer rooms I had been to, the balcony that overlooked the men's prayer room did not have a screened partition blocking direct sightlines between the two spaces. Instead, there was a very small marble and glass wall that went up about three feet, over which it was easy to peer down into the beautiful main prayer room, adorned with one continuous floral patterned blue carpet, a large chandelier, and a decorative blue mihrab facing Mecca. All around the interior perimeter of the mosque, at balcony height, were mounted arabesque inlaid wood pieces forming a diamond design. The openness of the balcony also meant that it was easy to see the worshippers down below. When we arrived, I could see two gentlemen laying green strips of fabric across the carpet in the main prayer room, facing the mihrab, a guide for where worshippers should place themselves to form equally spaced rows. Just in front of the strips of green, closer to the mihrab, was a prayer rug, where the imam would pray.

Kasey and I both explored the room within our own rhythms. She went toward one end of the prayer room and kneeled down, while I went toward the other, and took out my audio recorder and headphones to try and get a baseline recording level before the adhan began. I hit play and slowly increased the microphone gain until I could hear the sounds of the people and the space around me. It is always a bit of a guessing game to set levels for the adhan, as it is impossible to know how loud it will be until the muezzin begins. It is for this reason I try and take an educated guess, but always aim for slightly lower levels at first, so that the initial bit of the recording does not distort if the adhan is very loud.

There were a few women already in the prayer room, some in conversation while others sat quietly waiting or in silent prayer. There were also many children. Children running and laughing and playing and sitting on the silk carpets, staring at mobile phones and playing video games. At that moment, the soundtrack of the mosque was video game sounds up in the balcony, and men's voices down below where it seemed a Qur'an session was going on. I could hear one man chanting or reciting verses from the Qur'an, while the other men were gathered around him in a semicircle. Then, the reciter would chant a number of lines on his own, and the other men would respond in a call and response fashion. This reminded me a lot of Torah lessons and reading from the Bible. The reciter said his final line, and his chant naturally faded out. The men got up from the circle. Some dispersed and others began placing the green fabric strips on the carpet.

As the prayer lines were being laid, a young man in black jacket and black slacks walked up toward the mihrab with his hands grasped in front of him. I thought, perhaps he was praying silently for a moment toward Mecca. Then suddenly, the adhan began. I was focused intensely on the recording, trying not to move the recorder to avoid handling noise, but also to ensure that the levels were correct as the muezzin's voice vacillated dramatically throughout the first few verses. Once things were under control with the recording, I turned my gaze away from the main prayer room where men were beginning to gather and assemble on the green strips, and back toward the ladies' prayer room where I was kneeling on the floor.

There were now many more women entering the prayer room, all exchanging glances and smiles, and organizing themselves loosely in three rows across the length of the room. Most gathered nearer to the entryway, close to the balcony, looking over at the main prayer room. It took me a moment of observing, before I realized that most of the women were now standing and clad in a white and blue floral-patterned cover from head to toe. I was very familiar with traditional Muslim women's clothing from India and the Gulf, which was more typically the abaya—a black robe that was either one piece and placed over the head, or put on over the shoulders like a bathrobe and closed by tying, buttons, or a zipper. The abaya was worn over women's clothing for modesty. But these women were wearing something I had never seen before. The outer layer looked to my untrained eye a bit like a large bedsheet that they had placed over their heads and wrapped around them, or perhaps a beautifully patterned fabric, but they were all wearing the same one. Then images of nun's habits entered my mind, because of the way the material laid over their heads. Some women walked into the prayer room with this material in hand, and I watched them place it over themselves, while others walked into the room with it on (figure 15.1 and recording 18).

Once the adhan concluded, the women began to pray. I noticed that they all clasped the open part of the sheet at their fronts to form a closure. I later learned that the chador, the open piece of fabric or cloak the women were wearing, is a form of prayer cloth very commonly worn in Iran. Its distinctive characteristic is that it does not have a clasping mechanism, zipper, buttons, or snaps, but rather the woman wearing the chador will hold the garment closed with her hands. I learned from doing a bit of research that in present-day Iran, it is most common for women to wear a black chador when they leave the house, whereas prior to the revolution, black was reserved for funerals. In present-day Iran, colorful chadors, like the ones I saw inside the Copenhagen mosque, are most commonly worn inside the home.

96   *Chapter 15*

Figure 15.1   Imam Ali Moskeen, Copenhagen, Denmark.

I packed my audio recorder and headphones back into their pouch, discreetly, as to not interrupt the prayer that was beginning. Kasey and I caught each other's gaze and we both made our way to the door, down the stairs, and to the shoe racks, where we put our shoes and coats back on before stepping out into the cold. We walked back across the street to our bicycles, all the while discussing what a beautiful experience that was. Kasey was curious what it might be like to take her boyfriend to the mosque, recognizing that she and I had the ability to travel inside the space together as two women, but that if he came he would be in the main prayer room. I marveled at the beauty and elegance of the building while taking a few photographs of the exterior. We jumped back on our bicycles, I placed the audio recorder back into the basket and secured my gloves in place, and we rode off back to the apartment.

Recording #18   Imam Ali Mosque, Copenhagen, Denmark—Dhuhr Adhan.

PART III: REFLECTIONS BY KASEY KOZARA

By the time Diana took me to visit the Imam Ali Mosque in Copenhagen, I had been living in the city for two years. I came to Copenhagen from Abu Dhabi, and to Abu Dhabi from Dhaka, and to Dhaka from Northern India. All told, I had spent the previous decade in places where mosques, and the accompanying call to prayer, were a natural feature of the visual and aural landscape. To this day, I am fondly amused whenever I recall the adhan in Dhaka. It was always broadcast live, with a sort of layered texture as each successive loudspeaker was cranked up a second or two after the one before it. Invariably, the man giving the adhan would only launch into it after a full five minutes' worth of graphic throat clearing (also broadcast live). Contrastingly, Abu Dhabi's adhan felt solemn to me. Always synchronous, prerecorded, and pitch perfect. Majestic and soothing to the ears.

Moving to Denmark, I was painfully aware of the shift from warm Middle Eastern and South Asian climates. But until Diana took me to the Imam Ali Mosque in Copenhagen, I had not been conscious of the fact that the adhan had become a lost feature in my daily soundtrack. Given the choice, I would want it back. Churches are of very little interest to me, but I have sought out and visited several mosques over time. Some, like the Blue Mosque in Istanbul, required me to wind my way through the dizzying interior amongst hordes of other tourists and worshippers. I much prefer the times when I could slip in like an invisible observer. In reality, I probably scream, "outsider." But that's the thing. It has always amazed me how undisturbed mosque attendees are by my presence, or perhaps more accurately, how their doors are kept open to curious non-members like myself.

Arriving at the Imam Ali Mosque, with its blue mosaicked dome and minarets so uncharacteristic of Copenhagen, I wondered how Diana and I would be perceived and was very conscious of my not belonging there. I was relieved, and a little surprised, when the imam was so welcoming. I wondered whether his warm reception could have been a micro-form of community outreach, as it is my own sense that the Muslim community does not have it easy here in Denmark. While not citing Islam as their target, political parties as recently as 2020 have tried to ban "loudspeaker amplified prayer calls"[2] (i.e., the adhan). All this while the sound of church bells reverberates throughout the country. Having never even heard the adhan in Copenhagen over the past five years of my residence, I am not sure what all the fuss is about in the political sphere.

What I do know is that being inside the Imam Ali Mosque was like being transported far away from Copenhagen. Diana and I ascended a staircase to the women's section overlooking the main prayer room. A few women and their children were present and going about their business; the women devoted to praying and the children devoted to handheld gaming devices.

These kids represented a universal truth that regardless of what religion you subscribe to in your family, going to church, mosque, or temple leaves much to be desired if you happen to be a little kid. After settling ourselves on the floor atop some nice Persian carpets, Diana took out her recording device and set it up on the ledge of the balcony overlooking the prayer room. I recall feeling a little nervous, like we would offend or create anxiety with the electronic equipment, which was only discernible to a sound engineer. As it turned out, nobody paid us any attention, especially not those kids, absorbed as they were in their own electronic gadgets. Feeling at ease, I gazed down at the men bowing and prostrating below, vaguely aware of the minute sounds from video games and women's whispering from behind, and let myself take in the adhan filling the space around us.

Chapter 16

Making Scholarly Art

As an artist, I encounter the world first and foremost as a soundscape, a never-ending, always-intersecting, and at times sensually offensive, immersive aural experience. The idea for an exhibition made from the field recordings of the adhan had always been kicking about in my mind. I had one major hang-up with the idea, and that was the delicate complex negotiation between art and ethnographic research. Is it ethical to make art from documentation of cultures and communities of which I am not a part? I feel I have been chasing down the illusive answer to this question for most of my career. I have found myself exploring all angles of this question through projects and articles about art and archival materials, and about creative practice and sound recordings. This question was the focus of my dissertation, and is a question I pose to my students about their creative and narrative projects. As a scholar and artist, my work considers the intersections of these two arenas, and my creative practice and research interests are deeply intertwined.

It was inevitable that I would weave the recordings of the adhan into a creative project, as I am motivated intrinsically to make creative work. Moreover, as a scholar in academia, I know the importance of developing arts-based research methods and adding to the canon on creative practice. In fact, I feel that as a creative scholar, it is my responsibility to do this work because of a belief that creative practice helps to reveal new ways of thinking and knowing that are not accessible through intellectual inquiry and reasoning alone. These ways of knowing might best be described as being in our bodies, revealed and understood experientially. This knowledge is tied to the practice of doing and making, and is both powerful in its own right, and expands upon and deepens more traditional methods of inquiry.

In 2003, Peter Dallow argued that arts-based research methods need to be thought of like scientific methods, as critical elements to the expansion of artistic thought.¹ And in 2012, Florian Dombois et al. argued that artistic practice should be valued as research not for its methodologies or alignment with research in scientific disciplines, but for the unique contributions of creative research often absent in other disciplines.² The evolution of arguments for the purpose and value of creative research has been persistent and has slowly moved further from the traditionally constructed academic arguments about value, and toward a framework that dares to acknowledge that arts-based research creates knowledge differently. I would add to Dombois et al. and Dallow's arguments, that there is a distinct form of knowledge, intrinsic bodily knowledge, that comes from artistic research and practice. This knowledge is often acquired by both the scholar/practitioner as well as those that are audience to their work. It is because of this intrinsic bodily knowledge that creative practice and arts-based research endeavors have become critical modes for reflecting on, and making meaning of the human condition. Bodily knowledge is different from the type of intellectual reasoning and argument I have used in compelling academic colleagues to take new research seriously, or which I have asked of students when contextualizing their own ideas within those of others. In my experience, the knowledge we acquire in our body, be it from trauma, love, or intuition, stays with us and impacts the way we move through the world. I would argue that creative practice and arts-based research have the ability to create bodily knowledge and knowing in this same way. It is for this reason that I create art, and find it is critical to weave together my scholarly research and public-facing creative work. When I engage in creative practice, I learn intellectually as well as through my body, and the bodily knowledge impacts the way I approach the world. I make art from my research with the hope that the creative work can impact an audience on a bodily level. In 2014, I developed *Sonic Storyboard: A Call to Prayer*, which aimed to challenge visitors' assumptions and perceptions of the call to prayer.

The use of interactive media technology in the Sonic Storyboard project allowed me to incorporate aspects of the adhan and people's participation with it, into an exhibition targeting non-Muslims who are not necessarily familiar with the practices of reception.

The adhan is a recitation that demands participatory listening from Muslims.³ Listening to the adhan triggers practices of "reception" that are learned by followers of the faith. These practices of reception are interactive at their core. In "Islam, Sound and Space: Acoustemology and Muslim Citizenship on the Kenyan Coast," Andrew Eisenberg talks about this participatory practice in a Swahili Muslim community in Mombasa, Kenya. "Proper audition of the *adhan* implies an active process engaging not only the ears but also the entire body, including the voice. Upon hearing the first line, pious Muslims repeat the first words '*Allahu Akbar*' (God is Great) quietly to themselves, alongside with other prescribed responses to subsequent lines."[4] This mixing of participatory listening, with reactivity mediated by technology, is an important element of the Sonic Storyboard exhibit that runs beneath the surface, one which brings critical elements of listening and participation to the visitors' experience. I was excited to use my creative practice to further think through the research on the adhan, and to explore questions of the power of sound on bias and the role technologically-mediated interactivity plays in human participation.

Sonic Storyboard: A Call to Prayer is an ever-changing soundscape. Each time a person enters the gallery space, and their presence and movement in the space changes, what they hear changes. In other words, each person's mere presence in the gallery impacts the resulting soundscape that is heard by all visitors. This kind of technological mediation, where a person's presence changes the sounds in the space, intends to highlight the impact an individual's actions, and in some cases inaction, can have on other individuals and on themselves. The exhibit asks us how aware we are of this impact, and what we are willing to do about it once we are aware of our participation, however unwittingly, in impacting others' perceptions. The technological mediation of the recorded sounds is designed to provoke people to think about how their seemingly innocent presence and "mere observation" of the call to prayer actually augments the adhan, calling into question not only what they hear, but the very nature of listening and observation.

The exhibition also relied on a technique for decoupling and then recoupling visual and sonic material through technological mediation, as a way of evoking reactions in an audience. The exhibitions I have created that rely on this practice, assume that an audience is more visually oriented than they are sonically oriented. While this is of course not true of all people, I have found it is of many. Through this process, visual imagery and field recording are used to immerse the visitor in a multimodal environment, whereby the strategic placement of visual art-often photographs or screens showing photographs-and spacialized sound, creates a moment of simultaneously seeing and listening to a story. In a world where we are socialized into the immediate gratification of the watching experience, this way of exhibiting sound offers a decoupling of the visual and sonic, and an imperative for a recoupling that is defined by the user. The hope is that by asking the viewer/listener to participate in an exhibition where the visual and the aural tell a story that the audience must work to understand, one cannot help but participate and in turn engage with the work.

I wanted to exhibit this work in the Emirates but was not sure how well received the work might be. I thought about connecting with galleries, but at that time, there were very few small galleries that would be interested in such a conceptual piece about the adhan. I was also very new to exhibitions and was unsure about the nature and quality of my work, which I now realize made me hesitant to even speak about my exhibition let alone write to a gallery about it. Luckily, this block in myself did not halt the work from being shown. My girlfriend was moving to Singapore for a new job and offered her vacant apartment as a gallery space between when the movers came and when she had to turn the keys back into the management company. This felt like my opportunity to show the work.

Gallery 4211, the pop-up gallery where I mounted the first iteration of this exhibition, was a large empty living room space painted teal and light brown to echo the sand and the ocean of the city with great light in a prominent high rise near the corniche in the Khalidiya neighborhood of Abu Dhabi. The exhibition took place on May 23, 2014, and was attended by roughly forty people. The installation was up for a twenty-hour period with a formal opening at 5:00 pm. The opening was heavily attended, and it served as an opportunity to provide information on the objective and process of the project, which was communicated through a ten-minute introduction. This also served as an opportunity to explain and demystify the technology used in the exhibition. "I was interested in how collecting recordings and images of the call to prayer from different mosques, then synthesizing them into a contained sonic environment, could engage listeners to challenge their perception of the call to prayer, and spur dialogue around it."

The exhibition relies on the field recordings of the call to prayer I have made, four different speakers that were configured into a sound square around the gallery, and a series of software programs, cables, and hardware. A microcontroller sensor–driven data collection system was developed to take people's movement in the space as the impetus for a changing soundscape. To accomplish this, ultrasonic sensors were placed below each photograph in the gallery. These sensors collected data of people's movement in the gallery, and that data was sent through cables to an Arduino Uno microcontroller, essentially a tiny computer that fed the sensor data into a small program that was loaded onto the microcontroller. After the microcontroller reconfigured the data of people's movement into a form that could be read by another set of computer programs, the new reconfigured data was then sent by the microcontroller to a computer and fed directly into a small computer patch built in Max, a visual programming tool. The sensor data was read by the Max program and parsed into individual channels, each channel playing a different recording of the adhan. The Max program then used the constantly refreshing numerical data from the sensors in the gallery to dynamically control a number of sonic parameters that affected the playback of the recordings. These sonic parameters included pitch, amplitude, azimuth, and tempo. Each channel, with its unique recording, had one sonic variable that was impacted by the sensor data. In this way, the recordings of the adhan that were played back into the gallery through the sound square speakers were impacted by the changes to the sonic variables, which were created by the movement of the people in the gallery.

The Max patch was designed so that a person's interactivity or movement nearer or further away from the ultrasonic sensor (photograph of a mosque) would augment one of the predetermined parameters of the field recording. The intention behind these augmentations is that they create an obvious enough change to the recordings of the adhan to be noticeable to a listener. I was very interested in the audience eventually realizing how their movements impacted what they were hearing. This happened most effectively when there were only one or two people in the space, as the relationship between one's movement and the variation in the playback of the adhan was more tangible and distinctive. The exhibit drew attention to the relationship between the listener and what was being heard. Specifically, the exhibit made clear the way one's movement in the gallery impacted the resulting sound.

I spoke with a number of participants after the exhibit to seek their thoughts and experience of the work. The exhibition had many unintended outcomes, both on an artistic level, as well as with regard to audience experience. I discovered that through interaction with the recordings of the call to prayer, as well as physical interaction with the sensors and photographs, the visitors created an alternate sonic reality that was actually more haunting than the reality. This was not an intended outcome; however, I learned through interviews with visitors to the exhibit that it was a shared experience. When the exhibition space was empty, the adhan sounded beautiful. It was only when visitors walked into the space that the sounds became loud, jarring, and cacophonous. While I intended for exhibition visitors to hear the call to prayer in a new way, this project became a commentary on the role human beings play in augmenting our own and others' perceptions of what we hear. Our participation created a haunting sound, reminding us that listening isn't objective—our presence as listeners has the power to alter what we hear.

In June of 2019, I exhibited a second iteration of *Sonic Storyboard: A Call to Prayer*, at the Inter Arts Center (IAC), in Malmo, Sweden. The exhibition was tied to an artist residency I pursued at the IAC in the weeks leading up to the exhibition, and while similar in scope and nature to the original, this exhibition benefited from some major changes to the original programs. This second iteration focused heavily on making more seamless the human interaction with images in the space, this time on large screens placed throughout the darkened gallery. I focused on making changes that I hoped would allow the audience to develop more of a bodily knowing about the adhan, about listening, and about how our thoughts and actions impact our reception of Islam.

Chapter 17

Ezhara Beach, India, 2015

In late 2014, I took a semester leave from my job in Abu Dhabi to work on my doctoral dissertation. I spent the time living in Singapore, writing, catching up with friends there, and traveling for conferences and exhibitions. I was planning a trip to India late that December where I would hold my first joint exhibition with my artistic collaborator Dhanaraj Keezhara in Kannur, a city in the north of the southernmost state of Kerala. My friend Heidi wanted to come along for the exhibition, which was to start the day after Christmas. This motivated a Christmas excursion along the coast of Kerala for a few days before the exhibition began.

    I did some research and came across a guesthouse on Ezhara Beach. I emailed the guesthouse and received a response from the proprietor, Jacinta, saying that she did have one room available for our requested dates, and would require our payment upfront and in full to hold it. Ezhara, pronounced *air-ruhruh*, is a tiny coastal fishing village on the Arabian Sea, about thirteen kilometers south of the city of Kannur. There is a long sandy beach, rocky coast, a small town, and a large Muslim community there. The village has homes dispersed along the coast and narrow dirt roads that led to them, on which only three-wheeled auto-rickshaws and motorcycles could ride. Up on the cliff above the ocean, there are farms growing rubber, pepper, and nuts, stable crops in Kerala. We ended up spending Christmas 2014 with a British couple, their son who lived in Beirut and his girlfriend, Jacinta the proprietor, her maid, the maid's daughter, and the daughter's friend.

    There was no village center per se in Ezhara, but there was a sandy flat open area a five-minute walk from the guesthouse, where one could find a school, a mosque, and a large open-air concrete structure on the water where the fishermen would spend their time, and occasionally sell things. This village center was at the dead-end of the road and could be accessed by cars and small lorries. However, the one road that led to the village center was extremely narrow, and surrounded by water on both sides, so it was not easily traversable in the rain or in heavily inclement weather as the water levels would rise and cover the road.

The town mosque was a beautiful yellow color that aesthetically fit in well against the backdrop of the palm trees and fern mountain pass, up which school children would walk to access the main road and schools. One could walk up a footpath behind the mosque that served as a shortcut to the interior paved road above that ultimately led to the main street. The mosque itself looked old and weather-worn from being near the sea. It had mildew stain overtaking its exterior and roof tiles covered in moss, as did many of the structures in the area as the result of the mist off the water. Despite the aging and deterioration, there was something about the yellow minarets and the upstairs covered porch that made the mosque feel hidden and special. The area around the mosque was overgrown with natural vegetation, and there were some building materials nearby that suggested it was either undergoing repair or renovation, or that perhaps something else was being built in the empty lot in front.

To the right of the mosque was the dirt path that led to the mountain pass. There was a brick wall that defined the edge of the steps constructed into the path. I traveled down to the mosque my second day in Ezhara and sat on the brick wall with my audio recorder and headphones in hand. I had heard the adhan the previous days, though very faintly in the distance, and the amplification system was no match for the ocean waves crashing on the rocky shore out front of the guesthouse. I noticed that the bricks in the wall were overtaken with swarms of small red ants threatening to crawl through the mesh covering on my microphones. I jumped up. I had looked up the prayer times for Kannur, and had arrived with fifteen minutes to spare, hoping to hear the adhan. I didn't see anyone hanging out around the mosque, though there were many school children further down the dirt path toward the ocean, outside of the school that had likely just let out. On our drive to the beach house on the first day, I had noticed that there were many other mosques in the hill communities above, so I imagined this one catered to the immediate community. I waited for about thirty minutes recording the sounds of the environment, but I never heard the adhan.

We were given the top room at the Ezhara Beach House, which sounds luxurious, but in this case, by the time we reached the final wobbly narrow metal staircase to the roof, I realized that we may have a problem, or that Jacinta may have overbooked the house. The roof had a room built on top of it, big enough for a bed with a mosquito net and a standing fan. There was a bathroom directly across from the head end of the bed, the inside of which looked recently tiled but smelled dubiously old. The room had some concrete open shelves between the top of the walls and the ceiling, where odd things were stored and critters were likely hiding, and some gaps between the thin aluminum roof and the remaining walls. Outside of the room, there was a nice little sitting area with a plastic mat and a chair overlooking the ocean. We were definitely put in the room that was still being constructed but at least the view was beautiful.

The main house below us was a proper home with nice wooden doors and completed rooms. I managed to sneak a peek at the British couple's room. It looked finished and the walls met the ceiling. We survived the first night, though it was one of those falling asleep experiences where you forget, between the swatting away of mosquitos and the curious anxious glances at perceived signs of movement in the dark corners, when you were actually relaxed enough to close your eyes. Between things falling on the aluminum roof, the on and off noises of the water pump located outside our room that engaged anytime someone in the house turned on the tap or flushed the toilet, and the bugs and critters that we could almost see out of our peripheral vision, oh and the heat that one standing fan could not remedy, I was partially awake most of the night.

The next morning Jacinta suggested that we take a hike in the hills surrounding the guesthouse. She told us that the most beautiful beach in Asia was a twenty-minute hike, that way (she pointed to the left) along the coast. Muzhuppilangad was touted as the most beautiful beach because of its long black sand beach that is so hard that vehicles can drive out on it. We were intrigued enough to give it a go, so after breakfast and a quick visit down to the shore right in front of the beach house, we continued on for a hike. We began walking along the coast in the direction Jacinta pointed, all the while looking for the black sand. We got to a certain point where flanking the coast became difficult due to the rocky terrain. We stopped, and I broke out my Sony PCM to record the sounds of the waves hitting the rocks. It was beautiful and serene, and incredibly peacefully quiet for India. We continued walking up and over the increasingly larger-sized rocks—the further we went from the water—and into the trees. Eventually, after about forty-five minutes of walking, sweating and hiking, we reached high-lying ground from which we looked out hoping to see black sand. There was a rocky bend that blocked our sightline from seeing the black sand beach, so we decided to continue on at this higher elevation, figuring we might run into someone we could ask. As we tried to make our way, either to the black beach, which at this point I had given up on, or civilization, we stumbled through someone's rubber tree farm. It was muddy due to the rains, and we eventually dead-ended into a big dirt pile completely lost. Needless to say, we did not, despite our best efforts, find the black beach. However, we found our way back home by heading back along the coast from where we came.

Heidi collected a lot of shells on the walk, and I had a recording of the waves on the beach, which I incorporated into the fifth movement of the soundscape for the exhibition. Later that day, Jacinta hired an auto-rickshaw that took us and the British guy and his girlfriend to the black beach. Heidi and the British guy sat in the front, and the girlfriend and I sat in the back. I hadn't ever sat in the back of an auto rickshaw before, and I now know why. About ten minutes into the ride, my butt started burning up. We were sitting on several layers of cardboard covered by an old canvas banner, but the hot engine of the auto rickshaw was directly under us. I actually got up on my feet and squatted at one point, so that the soles of my flip flops could absorb the heat. We made it to the beach and the auto drove right up on it.

On Christmas Day, just before sunset, Heidi and I decided to head back down to the mosque for the sunset prayer. I again sat on the wall along the path with my audio recorder and headphones in hand, cautiously scanning the bricks for red ants. I switched the audio recorder on and listened through the headphones to the environment. There was a background drone of high-pitched crickets and other insects overlaid by the sounds of birds overhead—especially parakeets, dogs from nearby homes, the sound of vehicles passing and honking from the street up the mountain pass footpath, and of course, the very faint sound of the ocean. One might not even know from listening to the recording that the ocean is there, but if you do know, you can hear it. We were sitting on the brick wall and waiting for about fifteen minutes before the adhan sounded, and naturally we began to chat, as fifteen minutes is a very long time for two people to sit in silence without agreeing to do so in advance. But we whispered to one another so as to minimize the impact we might have on the recording if the adhan were to begin sounding when we were mid-sentence.

The adhan began. It was distant and melodic. It was coming from another mosque up the hill and was audible but in the backdrop of our soundscape, making passing cars and footsteps sound more audible than the adhan. It was a beautiful adhan. I hung on to the muezzin's voice through each phrase. We were both quiet as the adhan concluded and then looked at each other. You can hear a bunch of noise in the recording just after that first adhan concluded, which was me relaxing from a tense pose, where I used my arms to steady the recorder and not move its orientation to the source sound, and also me ensuring that my breath was calm so that it was not prominently featured in the recording. I then put the recorder down to scratch my foot.

We continued to sit on the brick wall and before I could stop fussing with the equipment another adhan began sounding in the distance, less than thirty seconds after the conclusion of the previous one. This one was even further in the distance over several hilltops and barely audible. We both sat quietly and tried to minimize the noises our bodies made interacting with the world around us, shoes digging into the gritty sand, and hands swatting away mosquitos. My left foot suddenly felt itchy, and I realized that while the red ants weren't out, the mosquitos were and in full force. We both started getting bit by mosquitos but held our ground. In listening back to the full recording from that day, I can hear the sound of us blowing the mosquitos off of us in an effort to not disrupt the recording of the adhan. Then just as the distant adhan was about to conclude, we heard a loud beeping sound coming from the mosque in front of us. It was a tinny twingey beeping that one might expect to come out of a motorized forklift as it is backing up. Then, the adhan began (figure 17.1 and recording 19).

Through the speakers of the old mosque the muezzin's voice was loud enough to carry the adhan to the beach, overpowering any other sounds around us. The speakers were of a poor quality, making it difficult to clearly hear the words of the adhan, even while knowing what to listen for. There was also a high-end feedback that was amplified along with the muezzin's voice. This was most likely the result of a high microphone gain paired with the muezzin standing close to the microphone during the recitation, likely with his mouth on or right up against the microphone. The high-end feedback sounded like an echoey high pitch that was most audible between

Figure 17.1 Mosque in Ezhara Beach, Kerala, India.

Chapter 17

Recording #19 Mosque in Ezhara Beach, Kerala, India.

phrases as the muezzin took a breath. As quickly as the adhan began, it ended. The muezzin's recitation was more in the tartíl style, with a steady mostly monomelodic chant that contrasted heavily with the two other adhan we had heard that evening.

    The moment the adhan concluded, I gave Heidi a glance and we both jumped up and moved away from the path, the mosque, and the overgrown vegetation where the mosquitoes of Ezhara seemed to make their home. We were both completely bitten up, Heidi mostly on her feet and me on my calves and shins. We quickly walked the five minutes back to the swath of sandy beach in front of the beach house, where we waded into the ocean, hoping the saltwater would help ease the itching sensation of the bites. Heidi continued her never-ending search for seashells, while I tried to keep my salwar pants and recording equipment dry. We headed back up to our penthouse room, displayed the newfound shells on the makeshift table on the porch overlooking the water, and changed into clothes for the Ezhara guesthouse Christmas Dinner.

Chapter 18

Protestors for Us

Sarasota, Florida, United States, 2016

In the winter of 2016, I traveled to Sarasota, Florida, to visit my friend Maggie. We reminisced about our time in Abu Dhabi, how we met, and caught up on life as we usually did once a year when I would visit.

Maggie and I became friends one hot summer day in August of 2010, when we took a Ramadan road trip with thirty of our colleagues from Abu Dhabi city to Fujairah. This particular hot summer day was a few weeks before students from all over the world were scheduled to arrive for the inaugural year of classes at New York University Abu Dhabi. That Thursday, we piled into four-wheel-drive vehicles and caravanned to the Rotana Resort in Fujairah. In 2010, August partially overlapped with the Muslim holy month of Ramadan when local law prohibits eating and drinking in public, and temperatures neared 120 degrees Fahrenheit or 50 degrees Celsius making for very hot road trip conditions. This trip to Fujairah, a mountainous emirate on the Gulf of Oman, was an attempt to escape the heat of the month, and as I saw it, a reward for all of the hard work we had done preparing to open the University.

The leader of the caravan brought his tan-colored FJ Cruiser to a stop, and all five people piled out of the car. The other seven cars followed suit and soon we were all scrambling to find shade under the few date palms that were clustered nearby. The rocks in the wadi were hot from the late morning sun, so we placed our beach towels under our bums and took out our packed lunches and water bottles as the call to prayer sounded from a nearby village.

I roped Maggie into coming with me to visit the Islamic Society of Sarasota and Bradenton, a ten-minute drive from her condo, where I hoped to record the adhan. We had decided to have a Jewish Christmas that year, a tradition I grew up with as a Jewish New Yorker, where you spend Christmas going to a movie and eating at a Chinese restaurant. Maggie and I went out to a dim sum restaurant for lunch, then headed to the mosque to catch the Asr Adhan, before the 5:00 pm movie.

As we turned into the driveway, we saw a large beautiful Moroccan-style mosque. The facade was a light sand color, and the front entrance, which was closed, boasted a four-poster dome archway. The parking lot was empty except for a light blue minivan in one of only three car spots near a side door entrance, which was unlocked and ajar. I wrapped a scarf around my head, put a light-weight sweater over my short-sleeved shirt and ventured inside the gate. The Islamic Center was designed around a large circular courtyard off of which visitors could access classrooms, offices, and the prayer rooms. I walked around the circle checking each room, hoping to find someone to speak to, perhaps the owner of the minivan. Maggie walked into the mosque at this point, and I explained that no one was there. I had identified the prayer room and noticed there were two speakers mounted at door height on either side of the main entrance, which I imagined were used to sound the adhan into the courtyard. As per my research on the prayer times for that day in Sarasota, which I cross-referenced with the mosque's website, I knew the adhan was meant to sound in ten minutes. Maggie and I sat on a stone bench in the courtyard, looking up at the blue sky and the way the prayer room dome glistened in it, waiting for the adhan. I had my recorder out and on, earphones in my ears listening to the amplified ambiance of the courtyard, waiting. Just as the clock struck 3:23 I heard it; "Allahu Akbar" [God is the greatest].

And then nothing. I waited, still as to not disrupt the recording with my footsteps, hoping the adhan would continue. After three minutes, I looked at Maggie and said, you did hear that right? I thought for a moment that maybe I had accidentally played back part of a previous recording on the audio recorder that only I could hear through the earphones. "Yes," she said. "But I guess that was it." It was a first for me. I had never before heard an adhan that just stopped. I wondered if perhaps the adhan was continuing inside but the amplification to the outdoor speakers was suddenly cut. I pressed my ear up against the prayer room door and heard nothing. The doors were locked so I could not enter and we still had not seen a soul, which is very uncharacteristic of prayer time at a mosque. I wondered if perhaps the adhan was a recording, which it did sound like, that was auto configured to not play that day. Or if it was manually switched off by the driver of the blue minivan as soon as it began. Perhaps there was no adhan because it was Christmas, or perhaps this mosque only sounded the adhan at certain times of the day. We walked back to the car, took off our headscarves and drove toward the movie theater.

The day after Christmas, we were headed to Naples, Florida for a barbecue with friends. I noticed that Naples also had a mosque, the Islamic

Center of Naples, which from what I could see on Google Maps, was a small storefront. I decided that I would try to record the adhan there. I drove directly to the mosque and arrived within minutes of the Dhuhr prayer time. The mosque was situated between a pizzeria and a taqueria. I put on my hat instead of a scarf this time and took my audio recorder out of the bag. At first glance, I did not notice any speakers outside the mosque, which wasn't a surprise given its location. The storefront had floor-to-ceiling windows over which green curtains hung to obscure the interior of the space from the public's gaze. I tried to open the door that read ladies' prayer room. It was locked. I walked over to the attached storefront, which I assumed was the men's prayer room, and attempted to open that door. It was also locked. I noticed a sign on the glass door that read: Jumu'ah (Friday Prayer) begins at 1:30 pm.

"I wonder if in Florida mosques only open for certain prayer times, or only open for prayer on Fridays?" I said to Maggie.

"That could be," she responded.

"I have never heard of that before," I said. "In all the places I have recorded the adhan so far, I haven't encountered a mosque that holds prayers only on Fridays. In fact, the only mosque I am familiar with that has prayer time only on holidays or special prayer days is my father's mosque in Brooklyn but that is because the community is small and primarily older, and there is no imam. The mosque functions more as a community center than a Mosque."

In Arabic, the word Al Jumu'ah means Friday as in the day of the week. In Arabic, the days of the week are named based on numbers. For example, Sunday, the first day of the week is al ahad, which is derived from waahid, the number one. Monday, the second day of the week is al aithnayn, derived from the word for the number two in Arabic which is ithnayn. Al thlaatha is Tuesday, derived from the number three thlaatha, and so on. This is true for all the days of the week with the exception of Friday, which is not derived from the number six, sitta, but rather the verb jama'a, which means to collect or gather. Al Jumu'ah, Friday, is the day of the week when all Muslims who are able, gather for the mid-day prayer. Whereas in many countries Friday is the last day of the workweek, in many Muslim countries the weekend includes Friday. In Saudi Arabia, for example, the weekend still falls on Thursday and Friday, and in the UAE, the weekend falls on Friday and Saturday, ensuring that Al Jumu'ah falls on a day when all can gather.

That Friday, I planned to return to the Islamic Society of Sarasota and Bradenton. I looked up the Jumu'ah Prayer time for Friday December 29th, in

Sarasota, which was at 12:32 pm. To be sure, I called the mosque that Friday morning and asked what time the Jumu'ah Prayer would be held. The man who answered the phone responded, "1:30 pm." "And the sounding of the adhan?" I asked? "1:30 pm," he repeated.

I borrowed Maggie's car and headed to the mosque. As I got close, I noticed a police car parked in the left-hand turning lane with its lights flashing. There was a police officer standing in the middle of the street with a reflective vest on. As I turned into the parking lot, the same one that was empty earlier in the week but was now overflowing with cars, I saw protesters holding signs and my heart sank. I paused and strained my neck to read the signs, concerned I might be walking into a politically or socially charged situation.

I notice that when entering mosques in the United States, I feel more uneasy and worried about how I might be received by the community than I do when I visit mosques in other countries, and of how protective and closed the communities might be toward me as an outsider. Yet, every experience I had up until that moment had debunked these concerns, as each community I had visited was kind and open. Perhaps, I was mapping onto the communities my own anxieties about Islam in the United States. Or maybe I wasn't, and I was picking up on a real and valid tension that was fueled not only by the complexities of being Muslim in a post 9/11 United States, but also by government policies and practices that were discriminatory toward Muslims like Executive Order 13769, more commonly referred to as the Muslim travel ban. The Executive Order, which was issued by Donald Trump and put into effect on January 27th, 2017 only days after he assumed the presidency, impacted entry into the United States by citizens of the following seven countries: Iran, Iraq, Libya, Somalia, Sudan, Syria, and Yemen.

The sign I could read said, "Reject Racism, Welcome Refugees!" The sign lingered in my mind. Was this an anti-refugee protest? Wait, welcome refugees? Was this a refugee welcome day at the mosque? Now I was totally confused. I parked the car in a grass spot in the rapidly filling parking lot and grabbed the little bag that held my audio recorder and headphones. I had a lightweight hat on fully covering my hair and a long sleeve outer garment to cover my arms.

Today, in contrast to my visit a few days prior, the front gate of the mosque was wide open. Families gathered to talk with other families in the entryway and others paused to take pictures out front of the mosque all dressed in beautiful outfits. I could tell already that this community was very different from those I had visited in large U.S. cities. This community was a mix of Muslims from many different cultural backgrounds, and the few people that I spoke to were not immigrants but had grown up in the United States. This community seemed affluent, and the Islamic Center was a striking architectural site complete with a beautiful bronze dome covering the masjid. I proceeded into the building, and this time there were people preparing for prayer and setting up an after-prayer lunch in the courtyard. It was 1:20 pm, so I headed directly for the ladies' prayer room entrance of the mosque.

The doors to the ladies' prayer room were now wide open, and there was a table and chair just outside where a woman in her mid-thirties sat. I approached the table, and said, as-salām alaykum greeting the woman, and introducing myself. The woman was lovely and greeted me with an ease and openness. I explained that I had come earlier in the week for the Asr prayer but that no one was at the mosque. She explained that all people come to pray for Jumu'ah Prayer as that prayer is compulsory. The other prayers some people come to but this one all people come to. This reminded me of the Jewish communities in which I was raised where people would conduct their own prayer and celebrations daily, some would attend synagogue services on Fridays for shabbat, but all would come together for certain religious celebrations throughout the year, like Rosh Hashanah and Yom Kippur.

I asked the woman posted outside the entryway if it would be okay for me to record the adhan either outside the mosque or inside. She said I was welcome to go inside to the ladies' prayer room. She also mentioned that if I wanted to speak with the imam, I was welcome to at the conclusion of the Jumu'ah prayer. I thanked her and walked through the doors. There, I removed my shoes and placed them in the floor-to-ceiling shoe rack. To the left was the bathroom where ablution could be performed, the ritual washing and purification of the body before prayer, if not already completed at home, and to the right was the staircase up to the ladies' prayer room. On the way toward the stairs, there was a door that opened into a small room with an all-glass wall, looking onto the men's prayer room where the imam speaks. I noticed that many older women were in this room, perhaps it was intended for those who were not able to climb the stairs to the upper prayer area. I proceeded upstairs.

Up until this point, I was not aware if I had visited mosques that did not recite the adhan five times daily. Though certainly, I must have. I never thought to ask a mosque this question as I had been so oriented to the UAE where prayer time was a routine part of daily life. So of course, I thought that every mosque held prayer time five times daily. I recall a conversation with a Muslim American colleague from the early days of my time living and working in Abu Dhabi. She, like myself, had worked at New York University in New York, before moving to Abu Dhabi. However, unlike me, she was a practicing Muslim. During my first Ramadan in the UAE, she and I got into a conversation about her experiences being a Muslim woman, working in New York versus in Abu Dhabi. One of the first things she said was that it was easier for her to be a practicing Muslim in Abu Dhabi, which while not surprising, left me curious as to why. She said that in New York, while many people including her boss knew that she was Muslim, that did not always mean that she was able to find time to leave work for prayer. And while there was infrastructure to support practicing Muslims, a makeshift prayer room in a hallway, it was not as conducive as those available at our temporary campus in Abu Dhabi.

> "What about Ramadan?" I asked. "How was it fasting in New York, when many people around you probably didn't even realize it was Ramadan. I was certainly one of those people," I said.

In the UAE, you couldn't not know that it was Ramadan. For starters, Ramadan meant that work came to a slowdown, as all government and private offices stopped work by 3:00 pm. We had office rules at the university that asked anyone not fasting to take all food or beverage into a windowless break room that was set up especially for Ramadan, rather than eating at their desk as they might do the rest of the year. And while all of the usual lunch spots around the city were closed during the daylight hours, most hosted beautiful elaborate iftar buffets for the breakfast at sundown each night. In the UAE, non-Muslims are legally required to follow the laws of Ramadan in public spaces, which means no eating or drinking in public during daylight hours. It was also the time of the year, when people had more road rage the later it got in the day, you could not get a taxi just before sunset as drivers were all pulled over waiting to eat their iftar meal that they had packed, and the malls were bustling between 12:00 am and 3:00 am just before the suhoor morning meal.

> "That was hard too," she said. "But the practice of fasting during Ramadan is a personal one, and it is okay if people offered me food not realizing or ate their lunch next to me. What was difficult was when it was near to time for the iftar, and I got called into a meeting or needed to stay back at work, those were the trying times."

The ladies' prayer room was large, with a beautiful rich red carpet that had individual prayer rug-sized designs of a mosque with a border that was meant to help signify the prayer lines and space for each person to pray, side by side. It was now only a few minutes to 1:30 pm. I took a seat on the prayer carpet against the back wall, where several other women were sitting. There were women who were upfront near to the glass overlooking the men's prayer area, some on their cell phones, and others chatting with friends. I exchanged smiles with a few of the women and their children, and the aunties to my right who were sitting in a row of chairs against the wall for back support. A little girl in jeans and a faded t-shirt, with plastic barrettes in her curly hair that reminded me of my childhood, took curious note of me as she walked past several times only inches away from my knees, all the time avoiding one aunty's cooing signs of affection toward her. I took out my Sony PCM recorder and my earbuds. I pulled up my phone's audio recorder as a backup and placed the phone face down on the prayer carpet against the wall and out of the way. I turned the audio recorder on and hit record. I dialed up the record gain level and down the headphone volume level and removed one of the earbuds to look less rude. It felt rude to be listening to music, what one would likely assume I was doing with white earbuds. Once the muezzin said his first Allahu Akbar, and I could properly attenuate the levels, and make final adjustments to the position of the recorder, I sat and didn't move until the call was over. Everyone else also sat at attention.

When it was over, the imam stepped up to the minbar, the pulpit from where he would deliver the Jumu'ah Prayer for the day, and gave a short reminder to the community.

He said, "I want to remind you that on all days when you come to pray, please come and wait for the adhan before you pray. Except for Jumu'ah Prayer, during the Jumu'ah Prayer you should come and begin to pray as soon as you arrive so that by the time the muezzin recites the adhan you can focus and pay attention to the sermon."

I hadn't ever been inside a mosque for a Jumu'ah Prayer before. I had heard the prayer amplified outside of mosques in Abu Dhabi, and seen people—always men, overflowing the prayer rooms of the mosques out onto the front stairs and into the streets, with their prayer rugs on Fridays. Women would never be seen praying outside. It would always be men in their white kurta pajama or kanduras with their skull caps, creating visual white waves of worshippers as they kneeled and stood (figure 18.1 and recording 20).

I would previously get up and leave the mosque after the recitation is completed. But this time, I stayed. I think I felt permission, because the woman at the counter outside the women's prayer room doors invited me. In fact, I am sure that I would have been welcomed to stay for the prayer at other mosques, but I had felt that I was intruding, falsely stepping, or participating in someone else's faith. The truth is I was suddenly curious what the imam was going to say. There was something about that first memo that he gave to the community of worshippers about when to pray for Jumu'ah Prayer that felt normal, familiar even. The concept of a spiritual leader, leading people in how to worship, and how to follow the rules of prayer, left enough space for me to feel okay not knowing how to be in the space. I stayed for the first ten minutes of the sermon and listened to what the imam had to say, and then I gathered my things and made my way back down the stairs to where I left my shoes.

As I passed through the threshold of the ladies' prayer room door into the courtyard, I noticed that it was empty. Everyone was inside listening to the imam. I momentarily considered if I should backtrack, turn around, take

Figure 18.1 Islamic Society of Sarasota and Bradenton, United States.

off my shoes, and head back up the stairs to the ladies' prayer room for the remainder of the sermon, after which I could head down to the courtyard to meet the imam. And then I remembered the post–Christmas holiday dinner I had agreed to help host at Maggie's place that evening, and the items I committed to picking up at the store on my way back from the mosque.

As I walked out the main gate of the mosque to the parking lot, I could see the people holding signs in the distance. I had temporarily forgotten about them when I was inside the mosque. There were two slender teenage girls in hijabs smiling and laughing under the shade of the driveway covering in the front entryway of the mosque.

Recording #20 Islamic Society of Sarasota and Bradenton, United States—Jumu'ah Prayer.

"Excuse me," I said. "I am a visitor to the mosque, and I noticed that there are people holding signs on the street, do you know what that is all about?"

One of the girls turned to me and said, "Oh yeah, they are like protesters, but for us."

"Oh," I exclaimed, never having heard someone explain something quite that way before.

"Yeah," she went on. "They are like protesting for our right to be here."

"Oh cool," I said, not sure what to say. "Was there a particular thing that happened at this mosque that the people are responding to?" I asked.

"No, nothing happened they are just always here supporting us," she replied.

I thanked the girls and continued walking toward the car. I paused, and thought, I want to go see what this is all about. I rerouted across the parking lot toward the main street where the "protesters for us" were stationed. There were still many people coming into the mosque for the prayer. At this point, the parking lot surrounding the mosque was full, and people were parking their cars in a lot across the street. The police officer, equipped with reflective vest and whistle, was stopping traffic on the main street to help pedestrians safely cross over to the mosque. As I approached the group, a woman, named Marcia, greeted me.

"Hello," I said. I introduced myself and explained I was visiting from New York and was curious about the signs and what they were protesting. I told Marcia I was an academic and that I visited mosques around the world doing research on religious recitation. Marcia, a Jew originally from New Jersey, was a member of Action Together Suncoast, the group that organized the advocates who held posters outside the mosque every Friday during Jumu'ah Prayer.

"We are a humanitarian group," Marcia said. "We focus on things that are being done by the current administration that are unconstitutional. As soon as the first Muslim ban was implemented, we decided that we would show our support outside of this mosque until whenever, and we may do it forever, who knows. It is our way of saying these are fellow human beings and these are members of our community, and we stand in support, and we are here every Friday and we will not put up with any bullshit. We have seen a wonderful trend of people honking and waving in support and joining us. To me, if you are a Muslim living in this country, you have already been attacked by virtue of the policies in this country. We are all in this together. We have been standing here for 48 weeks, every Friday at 1:00 pm we are here holding our signs. In four weeks, we will have been here for one year, the first year of this administration, and we will keep standing out here rain or shine."

I found Marcia and the group of supporters very interesting. I realized after a half hour of chatting with the group that this was something amazing. This group of people, primarily white, all non-Muslims and most over the age of fifty, spent every Friday from 1:00 pm to 3:00 pm showing their resistance against government policies they didn't agree with, by showing up for a community that had been targeted.

"We are very close with the imam of this mosque," Marcia told me. "We have dinner together; we have been invited to many events. We have a very close relationship beyond us standing here. We want to show the world that the only thing to be afraid of is what we don't understand. Educate yourselves." Then, she said, "Would you like to take a picture of us and send it to your Muslim friends around the world, and say look, not everyone is Trump?" My heart smiled.

"Sure." And I photographed the group. "Thank You, thank you for doing this," I added. An older gentleman from the crowd added, "We shouldn't have to be doing this but until the world changes markedly, we will be out here."

Figure 18.2 Members of Action Together Suncoast (ATS) Holding Signs, United States.

"I can tell you that this is the only Mosque of all I have visited that has had people outside protesting against government policy," I said (recording 18.2).

"That made our day," said Marcia. "In the summer when it is 95 degrees out here, the members of the Mosque bring us cold drinks and food, and people who have come to worship are handing out ice cream. When we have come for dinners, we would inquire about which foods are appropriate for us to bring. So this is a learning experience. We have never been treated with anything other than love and kindness."

There was something very familiar about my experience visiting the Islamic Center of Sarasota and Bradenton that day. It was community and family oriented. From the "protesters for us" group who comprised people from all walks of life and their children, who wanted to spend every Friday for an hour or two standing with signs promoting peace and love, to the families that pulled up to the mosque in their minivans and SUVs. There was an intergenerational feeling of community, where kids were running through the courtyard, teenage girls whispering to one another through their braces and with their cell phones glued to their faces. And embarrassing family photographs were being taken of children with their parents, leading to snapshots of beautiful flowing garments and awkward smiles. It felt American. A word I rarely use and can barely describe, there was something fundamental about my experience that day that was familiar beyond religion or language, and it was that it was culturally American.

Chapter 19
The Sonic Context

When I began this research project, I was aiming to capture a wide variety of recordings of the adhan, thinking that this would reveal a type of nuance about Islam that is often missing in Western notions, coverage, and understanding. I wasn't entirely certain what I meant by nuance at that time but felt showing a broad representation of Muslim communities was important. I had an idea in my mind that each recording of the adhan might be different in some way. I imagined that there would be a variation in approach and style from muezzin to muezzin and that recitation styles would glean influence from the local language and possibly musical traditions of the place. And before doing extensive research, I hypothesized that the adhan would sound different in different parts of the world.

As it turns out, there are sonic differences and nuances revealed through the recordings of the adhan, and no two are the same. In some cases, there is tremendous sonic nuance from muezzin to muezzin, and from geography to geography. By this, I mean not only that a recording made at one mosque is different from a recording made at another, but that there are unique aspects of the muezzin's recitation and the community itself that become embedded in these recordings contributing to these differences.

In all of the mosques where I have recorded, the recitation of the adhan has been impacted by the aesthetic stylistic choices and preferences of the muezzin. In some mosques, there were several muezzins within one community, each of whom would take turns reciting the adhan, each with their own distinctive voice and style. While visiting the mosque in Reykjavik, Iceland, Imam Ismaeel, after having heard the description of the soundmap project, suggested I might want to record an Icelandic member of their community reciting the adhan rather than another muezzin who emigrated from outside the country. His rationale was that when the Icelandic man recited the adhan, he brought a certain Icelandic folk quality to the recitation. It was as if the imam, unprovoked by the project motivation, was saying that the Icelandic man's recitation of the adhan was in some way sonically influenced by his Icelandic heritage and upbringing. Since I do not have a background in Icelandic culture, I can't say. However, I could tell in the process of recording the adhan and through listening back to it afterward that there was something very unique in the Icelandic muezzin's recitation style, namely tonal qualities and inclinations that I had not heard before. Which begs the question, if each muezzin brings his own background to his recitation style of the adhan, is a recording of an adhan sonically descriptive or unique to the place in which it is recorded, nuanced in its capturing of cultural information about the muezzin who recites it, or is it perhaps something else?

If you listen closely, you can quickly identify diverse variations and nuance in the recordings on the soundmap of the call to prayer. Through the course of this project I have determined that there is no one reason for this, but rather a variety of interconnected pieces that sculpt what and how we hear these adhan and the supplementary data, as well as the development of the sonic qualities of place within them. Cultural background and the muezzins' own reference points for recitation, including recitation styles they may have grown up with, become accustomed to, or have a preference for, are factors that contribute to the sonic nuances one can hear in these recordings. There are, however, three other key factors to consider when you listen to these recordings. These include (1) the sonic qualities of the place in which the adhan is recited—by this I mean the resonant qualities of the space, and how much echo or reverb there is due to reflective or absorbent surfaces in and around the mosque as well as other environmental and human-made sounds; (2) whether or not an amplification system is used either inside or outside the mosque, and the quality of that amplification system; and (3) the position and orientation, both physically and with regard to familiarity, of the recordist to all of the above when making the recording.

In addition to nuances in these recordings based in the muezzin's recitation style and the acoustics and sonic characteristics of the space in which it is recited, there is nuance that comes from the sonic context of the community. This approach to thinking about sonic contexts shares something with the ideas of sociologist and soundscape researcher Jean-Paul Thibaud, who says, "When we try to understand the way an atmosphere is generated, we have to consider the interaction between the built environment and the social practices it enables and relies on."[1] I like this way of thinking about the human, environmental, architectural, and social factors outside of the muezzin and the mosque that influence the sounds that can be heard in recordings of the adhan. Because the sonic context provides reference points that are specific to the community in which the recording is made, these reference points become indicators of an adhan recorded in that specific place.

These sonic points of access can orient the listener to a place through the captured resonances of the unfolding of everyday life. Thibuad suggests that this includes taking "into account the everyday activities of city dwellers."[2] While this may seem obvious, it points to something quite fundamental to recording, which is that gradual differences in behavior and environment can lead to strong sonic variation and contrast when recorded and reamplified. In Singapore, for example, this might mean the everyday sounds of people walking in the downtown speaking any of a multitude of the national languages including, Mandarin, Malay, English, and Tamil, running and biking through the park connectors, and coming together at hawker centers for mealtime. In Abu Dhabi, where I began this research, it might mean the sounds of rapid urban development: the construction of skyscrapers and the demolition of old buildings, the roar of luxury cars flying down the corniche, a menagerie of languages representative of the 80 percent expatriate community, and amidst this all, the call to prayer emanating from the mosques minaret's five times daily.

Further to the sounds of the human experience in urban contexts are the sounds of the natural environment both in cities and outside of them. Thibaud explains in his description of how ambiance unfolds that, "sound is . . . the result of an action. This can apply . . . to natural events like when the wind blows or the rain pours, rendering audible some features of the environment that were silent until then . . . [giving] access to what is happening."[3] Recording such moments of "action" also renders audible features of a place that may otherwise have remained unheard and allows us to capture and differently consider how sonic ambiance unfolds under particular circumstances. These circumstances, in addition to those named earlier, are what create the sonic contexts that you hear in these recordings. Culture and tradition, both felt and remembered, are crucial to ambiance. Consider, for example, the role quiet plays in recordings made in Scandinavian cities that prize a culture of quiet, or the way honking as a cultural norm impacts ambiance in recordings made in countries like India. Therefore, to capture the recitation of the adhan is not only the act of recording the adhan itself but also the sonic context of place.

Thibaud suggests a way of listening that distinguishes between "the way we interpret, recognize and understand the world we perceive," and "the way we feel and relate to the world we sense." He advocates in this context for "sensing rather than perceiving."[4] This book is in a way a manual for listeners of the soundmap, written to guide one through the process of listening to the recordings of the adhan. Through the audible and in this case the written, the book attempts to make visible the relationship between what we interpret and understand about Islam through our own perceptions of the world around us, and how we feel and relate to the world we sense through listening to the recorded adhan and the sonic contexts therein. In other words, the sonic contexts of the Muslim communities I have visited, which reveal themselves through the recordings made of the adhan, are an attempt to offer an alternative perspective on Islam that is to be felt and related to by a listener. This is the bodily knowledge I mentioned earlier on, and through creative research I am attempting to pass this knowledge onto readers. By offering the recordings on the soundmap, curated through the common thread of the adhan, a listener is challenged to consider how they feel and relate to the communities revealed through the sonic contexts that have been captured in these field recordings. Of course, the obstruction of listening between the lines of the adhan provides a very particular frame and conditions in which to consider the sonic context, leaving the listener to focus on details that may otherwise go unheard. To better understand the impact of these obstructions on a listener, one must simply listen to a recorded adhan on the soundmap, and then to another, and then another. The nuance of each adhan, as well as the variation and unique attributes of the sonic context, reveal themselves in technicolor to those listening to the recordings.

While eating dinner at a rooftop restaurant in Abu Dhabi one evening, I was pleased to hear the Isha'a (evening) Adhan in the distance. The sound was beautiful, large, and full. I shortly realized that I was hearing the adhan simultaneously from different mosques, all having begun at different times creating incredible counterpoint in the air. The following day, I returned to the same area of the city, but this time at street level. Standing alongside a major intersection in the downtown, beside the restaurant where I dined the night before, I could see three different mosques within a 100-foot radius. I attempted to record the Maghreb Adhan, but the sound was dramatically different from what I had heard the night before. At street level, I could hear one dominant recitation and one recitation faint in the background, both flanked by cars honking and street sounds, and I noticed that one of the mosques at the intersection was not in use. The recordings I have made of the adhan in Abu Dhabi are all different, despite the fact that the recitation is identical as it is broadcast over radio from the muezzin at the Grand Mosque. The particular mosque and amplification system they use, the part of the city where they are located, the time of the day, the time of the year, the position from which one is listening, and even atmospheric conditions impact the resulting soundscape of the city and the recordings that are made of these sonic moments.

I would argue that the process of recording the adhan changes the purpose and the meaning of the call to prayer from a religious recitation into a recording of a sonic context. If this is the case, then what do these recordings provide to a listener? In his essay "On Sonic Spaces," Paul Demarinis references the early phonographers' experiences of listening back to recordings on foil and wax cylinders as the origin of sound art, soundscape, sound sculpture and sound design. He explains that when phonographers recorded one sound, three could be heard. The first was the sound itself, the second was inadvertent sounds of the environment, and the third was the sound of the recorder or machine noise.[5] Exploring the use of noise in composition was the entry into deeper philosophical inquiry of what music is, what sound is, how they relate to one another, and the experience of hearing through composition.

I wonder what Demarinis would say is the relationship between the sounds we intend to record and those sounds and noises that we capture inadvertently. The inadvertent sounds become an equal part of the recording and are heard as a part of the sonic scene that a person envisions while they are listening back to the recorded sound. And so the recordist, the person who chooses what to record and from where—who for example positions their body toward or away from particular loud noises, who places the recorder above, below, or to the side of the thing they are recording—that person is making choices that change the resulting recording and impact what is ultimately heard. Had I, for example, chosen to record that Isha'a Adhan from the rooftop restaurant, the sounds of cutlery on dishes, wind, the soccer game on the large screen television in the background, shisha being smoked, and the noises made by other restaurant goers would become a part of the recording. And when I went down to the street level the following day to record the adhan, the ambiance of the place was completely different. That recording included the sound of cars driving through the megablock and on the main road, people walking, daily street life, and reflections of the simultaneous amplified adhan resonating off of the ten-story concrete buildings giving the listener the sense that one mosque was closer to the recorder. Though the two recordings could be of the Maghreb Adhan recited by the same muezzin, they would document different exchanges and parts of daily life.

By listening to the recordings on the soundmap and in this book, I intend for the reader to find themselves immersed in new cultural contexts and geographies, and to consider each given geography from a sonic vantage point, one largely devoid of the bias that often accompanies visual representations of Islam. By this, I am speaking specifically of the stereotypical and cliché visual portrayals of Muslims by Western media that are often conflated with terms like terrorism and refugees. Appropriate counter portrayals and representations of Muslims who are not living amid war and who do not claim Islam under a fundamentalist guise are not as widely represented as they should be. The result is the creation of a complex biased visual representation of Islam and Muslims that has been propagated to a wide audience. It is for this reason that communities, like my family's mosque in Brooklyn, New York, have been afraid for their place of worship to outwardly contain visual cues of their faith, and have until very recently chosen to avoid having any online presence. Perhaps listening to the sound recordings of the adhan might allow a listener to hear and internalize new narratives and knowledge about Islam.

Chapter 20

Bangalore, India, 2010

From August 2007 to June 2008 I lived in India. I split my time between Bangalore, a large city in the southern state of Karnataka, and Delhi, the National Capital Territory in the North of India. I moved to India after receiving the William J. Clinton Fellowship, a program through the American India Foundation (AIF) that pairs young Americans who have interest in the development sector with Indian NGOs. I was assigned to work for AIF's Digital Equalizer Program, a philanthropic initiative through Adobe that brought media making tools and curriculum to government school children in India. The sleeper train ride between the two cities is forty-two-hours long, and the trip by plane is two and half hours. I had a room in a flat in each geography, and two lovely roommates who would hold down the fort while I was working in the opposing city.

The project I worked on, Adobe Youth Voices (AYV), was simultaneously launched in Delhi and Bangalore, and I was on the project team that implemented the rollout. I spent more of my time in Bangalore than in Delhi, and really hit it off with my colleague there, Chandan. He was a year younger than me and had been born and raised in Bangalore, with a large family and a lot of knowledge about the city. He would often pick me up from my apartment in Malleshwaram on his two-wheeler, and we would weave through the traffic on our way to one of the fifteen AYV schools, many of which were on the outskirts of the city. Bangalore, as it has been explained, was a small hill-station town known for cooler climates in the hot season and has become a huge bustling city overflowing its seams. When I lived there, it could easily take an hour and a half to get from one side of the city to the other in an auto-rickshaw, and slightly less on a two-wheeler.

Chandan's family lives in Vijayanagar, which is twenty minutes from the apartment where I stayed near 15th Cross in Malleshwaram. He also has a number of cousins who lived closer to me in Rajajinagar, only a twelve-minute auto ride from my place. The Rajajinagar House, as he called it, is a three-story house occupied entirely by Chandan's extended family. There is a Hindu mandir on the top floor and a number of apartments below.

Chandan and some members of his family are followers of Sathya Sai Baba, the now-deceased Indian guru known for his large afro and often photographed wearing a long orange robe. Chandan's uncle was a devotee and erected a mandir to Sathya Sai Baba on the top floor of his house. Every evening around 7:00 pm, Chandan, his brother, and many of their cousins would assemble in the mandir at the uncle's house. They would chant devotional ragas and pray to Sathya Sai Baba, whose full-length photograph was mounted on the short back wall of the rectangular room, between two stately chairs; his uncle would sit in one of the chairs and the other held a large portrait of his deceased wife.

I began studying sitar with this uncle's son, Nishcal, who is several years younger than Chandan and an excellent musician. Nischal's primary instrument is tabla and was at the time seriously studying sitar as well. I had always been interested in studying Indian musical systems and instruments, and at that time I didn't know about the differences between the Hindustani and Karnatak systems or much detail about the musical instruments. I did know about the rigor and intense practice regimes that Indian youth were required to follow when studying music at private homes in Bangalore, and I did know that many serious musicians had a guru with whom they studied for many years.

Chandan and I spent most of our workdays together, traveling to and from government and NGO-run schools, and at times visiting the American India Foundation office on MG road in the heart of Bangalore. Our jobs were to get the youth media making program up and running, including dealing with the local politics that made this difficult to do. Chandan handled most of the politics in Kannada, the local language of Karnataka.

Our task for the year-long launch of the program was as follows. We were to develop an India-specific curriculum, hold teacher and student trainings, and ensure that schools had proper technical infrastructure to support the program, including computer hardware and software, solar panels and uninterrupted power supplies, and a BSNL telephone line so that the computer labs could have access to the internet. We were responsible for simultaneously building the infrastructure for the program, getting schools on board, and launching the curriculum in schools—all while keeping the program moving along toward the end of year mela where students were to showcase their final films.

Initially, I would study sitar with Nischal one or two times a week. After work, Chandan would offer to take me to the Rajajinagar house where

Nischal lived, and I would spend one to two hours in a lesson. This would often be broken up by a coffee break and then toward the end of the second hour, we would move into the daily bhajan upstairs in the mandir. As time went on and I became more invested in studying the sitar, Nischal offered to spend even more time teaching me. Often, I would spend three to four days a week studying sitar after work. I would arrive at Nischal's house sometime after his classes were over since he was in college, and we would spend several hours each lesson learning about the sitar. We covered the basics of the string arrangement, the fret system, the different tunings, the shruti box accompaniment, and how to tune the thirteen sympathetic strings, which required an entire week.

Nischal taught me about the Sa Re Ga Ma musical system, and we collectively tried to equate the Hindustani conventions to those of Western music, which he had great interest in. He taught me about the ragas, how there are many ragas, and how some are for morning and others for night. He taught me how to read musical notation for the sitar, but mostly I learned by rote memorization. He would play something on his sitar, and I would need to play it back. I would practice thip tuck strumming techniques, while gaining speed moving the pre-coconut oiled index finger on my left hand across the top string, and he taught me how to bend the strings to form a type of vibrato and for pitch bending purposes. I came for the sitar lessons, drank the coffee, and stayed for the bhajans. Nishcal was on the path to becoming my guruji.

The bhajans are devotional and extremely musical. Nischal often played the tabla and Chandan the harmonium, and the group of cousins sat in rows facing the uncle who sat erect in his chair against the wall beside the full-length portrait of Sathya Sai Baba. We sat on the floor cross-legged and sex-segregated with an aisle between us, women on the right and men on the left. There were often seven to ten people in the mandir. Chandan's extremely musical family would chant ragas and devotional melodies in Sanskrit, some of which I began to recognize over time but none of which I can name. I learned when to clap along, but mostly, the experience was like being in the synagogue as a child, reciting along with prayers whose transliterations I could read but whose meaning I could not follow.

In 2010, after moving to Abu Dhabi for a new job, I used my first vacation to travel back to Bangalore to see Chandan and his family. It had been two years since I lived there, but things seemed very much the same. His father took us all out to the Central Tiffin Room (CTR), a small hole in the wall restaurant in Malleshwaram with unarguably the best butter masala dosa in the world. Nischal was still playing the tabla and the sitar, Chandan was still riding his two-wheeler, and the bhajans were still prominently featured at the end of most days. I was only in Bangalore for a few days and in addition to spending time with Chandan and his family, I had two goals. The first, to buy a small carved wooden elephant with inlaid mother of pearl as a sixtieth-birthday present for my mother, and the second, to record the call to prayer.

I had a clear idea of where in Bangalore I could find the elephant. There was a nice shop on MG Road with many beautiful items that I had visited when I lived in Bangalore, but which at the time I could not afford. Chandan traveled with me to the store, and I found the elephant I was hoping to purchase, a small but solid beautifully decorated hand-carved piece of artwork that my mother would eventually name Eleanor Rigby. The shop, a hotspot with tourists, was well versed in shipping items around the world for their customers. However, the shipment costs to get Eleanor Rigby from Bangalore to New York were as much as her ticket price, and so Chandan and I decided I would carry her on the plane from Bangalore back to Abu Dhabi. He loaned me a khaki-colored gym bag made of sturdy canvas material that we could fully zip up around the elephant after removing her tusks, and which I eventually years later returned. I succeeded in bringing her back to Abu Dhabi with a bit of shoulder pain from the weight of the bag. She took up residence for seven months on the living room floor of my Abu Dhabi flat between a potted fern and the antique wood cabinet. I did eventually carry the elephant back to New York on a fourteen-hour flight and presented her to my mother. Eleanor Rigby now resides atop a wooden dresser in my mother's bedroom in New York alongside a much larger white horse from China who remains nameless.

In 2010, I was not yet well-versed in recording the adhan and was still navigating how best to track down a local mosque, how to identify the prayer times, and how much preparation time I needed. I asked Nischal and Chandan if they knew of a mosque near to the Rajajinagar House where we spent a lot of our time that visit. I could tell from Nischal's expression, he was a little thrown by the request and curious about why I wanted to go. Despite growing up in Bangalore, neither was very familiar with the location of local mosques, which is not all that surprising given how religiously segregated Bangalore is. There was a mosque connected to one of the schools that Chandan and I had worked at in 2007, which he suggested I try.

I traveled to the mosque which I remembered from my many visits there while rolling out the AYV program. I had distinct memories of this school and the teacher who partnered with the AYV program. This was an all-Muslim school attached to a mosque, and the teacher was a devout Catholic who wore a chain with a cross on it prominently displayed on top of her sari. I also had fond memories of the students I worked with there and one young boy in particular who was extremely interested in being the boom operator for their documentary film project. I climbed up a few steps to the corner snack shop across the street from the school and mosque, purchased some fried banana chips and waited. I prepared my recording equipment and tried to casually perch against the metal railing in the mid-day sun while listening through headphones to multiple conversations between the shop's proprietor and folks coming in for a cold drink or a chai. After waiting a long time, well past when the Dhuhr Adhan should have been recited, I packed up my gear. I asked the shop owner about the adhan, and he said maybe at 3:30 pm, which meant perhaps the mosque only sounded the adhan for certain prayer times each day. I was disappointed and very hot by that point. I hopped into an auto-rickshaw and headed back to Chandan's house.

It was my last day in Bangalore, and I hadn't yet even heard the adhan in the daily soundscape of the city, let alone recorded it. I asked Chandan's brother if he had any idea where there might be a local mosque, and he suggested I try a mosque in Rajajinagar not too far from the house. At my request, Chandan and Nischal dropped me off at the mosque forty-five minutes before prayer time.

Masjid E Noor was large and mostly white with green accents on the trim and minarets. There was a beautifully adorned locked steel gate at the entryway through which I could see a small interior courtyard and beyond that wooden doors that led into the mosque. Masjid E Noor was on an interior road that fed into a small traffic circle, where several roads convened but where no formal traffic patterns existed. I stood toward one edge of the circle and took out my small handheld audio recorder with a fuzzy windscreen on top to block the pressure disruptions from the wind. There were two-wheelers and auto-rickshaws whizzing by. I started cautiously, aware of my surroundings and not wanting to unnecessarily draw attention to myself. Luckily, there weren't too many people in the traffic circle, most were passing through and stared but kept moving along. I put in the earbuds, which I used instead of the large over-the-ear headphones to be discreet. After five minutes with no one approaching me or questioning me, I became more brazen and held the recorder above my head to move the microphones out of the direct path of the honking horns, which were plentiful and difficult to listen to amplified by the microphones. I moved around the perimeter of the traffic circle trying to find quieter spots to record from, but the entire area was noisy.

Diagonally across the circle from the mosque, there were a few large buildings with shops in them. I walked to the shops hoping there might be somewhere to have a chai, or a stoop to sit on and think up a plan for my next steps. It was mid-day and many of the shops seemed closed, which was not uncommon in India. I walked up a few steps to an exterior first-level balcony of one of the buildings and saw a sign for a video shop. I thought the store might carry AA batteries which I was trying to stock up on, as my audio recorder required them and was running low. While the main door of the video shop was open, I didn't see anyone inside when I entered, and noticed that there was a sheet tied up in the threshold just behind the counter that led to the back area. I had known many shops in Bangalore that were multipurpose and served as people's homes in addition to their business. The interior of the shop was built like an older home with very small dark rooms, which helped the space stay cool on hot days. There were large glamour shot blowups and portraits on the walls, many of children, some with bright and elaborate backgrounds. As I was deciding whether to stay or go and perusing the items on the wall behind the counter for batteries, a middle-aged man walked through the curtain and said hello.

"Can I help you?"
"Hello Ji, I am looking for some batteries."
"What kind of batteries?"
"I am looking for Double A, do you carry them?"
"No. We carry more lithium batteries."
"Okay," I said.

I continued to stare past the gentleman and through the curtain that he left pushed to the one side when he entered to store. I noticed that just beyond the curtain, there was a small alcove room with several antiquated television monitors and a video camera sitting on a desk. It looked like a video editing station.

"You were the one out there before, were you?" he asked.

A woman in a nighty or South Indian home dress walked out from behind the curtain and said, "Yes, you were out there with that fuzzy thing." "Yes," I smiled. "I was recording some audio sounds." "What kind of sounds?" she asked. "I was recording some sounds of traffic, and autos, and honking and also some birds," I replied. The woman's questioning put me at ease, and I asked what they did in this shop. She and her husband, as I learned, ran the video shop, which offered a variety of services from photographs to marriage videos. They lived behind the shop with their two school-aged daughters. I took out my audio recorder and explained that it was a self-contained audio recorder with stereo XLR input options. He asked me how much it cost in Rupees and where I got it from. He talked to me about some of his camera gear and audio equipment that they use on their shoots. He told me that it was difficult to find the kind of recorder that I had on the Indian market and that it was too expensive to take it from another country. I handed him the recorder to examine, and he listened to some of the recordings I had just made in the traffic circle. While we were talking, their daughters came home from school. I nodded a hello as they ran back behind the curtain with their school bags.

At this point, I knew that the family was Muslim. There were a few indications in their business and home, primarily the absence of any Hindu statues or imagery, which was a staple in most Hindu-run businesses. But also, the man and woman spoke in Hindi to one another and their children, which in Bangalore I had learned was most common with Muslim and North Indian families, whereas Hindu families from Karnataka traditionally spoke in Kannada at home. I had learned this through my reliance on auto-rickshaws for travel around the city. The Kannadigas, or natives of Karnataka, would never understand my haggling in Hindi or my questions or directions, whereas the Muslim drivers always did. There was also the fact that the older daughter was wearing a hijab when she came home from school.

I asked them if they could tell me when the prayer time was and asked if they knew if the adhan would be sounded outside the mosque. I asked if we could hear it from their shop. They said yes and confirmed the time, which was more than an hour later than what I had thought it was. I explained that I wanted to record the adhan, and they said I could sit in the front parlor of their shop to stay cool until it was prayer time.

I thanked them and sat on the front step of the shop, leaning into the cool of the room for a while. As the prayer time neared, I felt a slight anxious pang in my chest, knowing I was going to need to navigate another conversation and another explanation as I neared the mosque with my audio recording equipment. I contemplated recording the adhan from the shop but knew the traffic noise from the circle would be too overpowering. I figured my best bet was to get somewhere up high above the traffic to record. I left the video shop and walked around the traffic circle to the mosque to take a few photographs. I peered in through the main gate, which was still closed, to get a better sense of the interior.

A man walked out from the gate of the mosque and approached me with impeccable English.

"Hello, can I help you?"
"Hello," I said.
"Are you Muslim?" he asked.
"My father is Muslim," I replied.

What I withheld of course is that I was raised Jewish and more strongly identified with the Jewish faith, but I knew that would further complicate things, and possibly make it difficult for me to communicate the nature of my interest in the mosque. He went on to introduce himself as a doctor in the community and the president of this mosque.

"I have seen you taking photographs here. What are they for?" he asked.

Directness was in my experience a very Indian quality, and while I was somewhat on guard, I answered him. "I am doing a project," I said. "I am interested in recording sounds and taking photographs of mosques from different places, and then using them for a project." He asked me a few more questions, and I asked him when the adhan would sound. He told me that if I wanted to come inside the mosque for prayer, I could, and he welcomed me.

In retrospect, I should have gone inside, though I would not have prayed, and I was worried this might create an awkward situation that at the time I didn't know how to navigate. I would have liked to meet members of the community, see the mosque and learn a bit more about the Muslim community within Rajajinagar, a neighborhood I knew so well through Chandan's eyes and those of his Hindu family. Instead, I thanked him but declined. He told me that if I wanted to speak to the muezzin, I could. The doctor disappeared back behind the gates of the mosque and fifteen minutes later the muezzin came out and said hello. The muezzin was a young man with a long beard. Unlike the doctor, his English was very limited, more on par with my Hindi skills. So, we mostly smiled at one another while the doctor did the explaining. The muezzin talked a little bit about what he does, and how many times per day he recites the adhan. He told me about how long he had been a muezzin and that he was from Bangalore.

He wore a simple white kurta pajama and a skull cap. The same kind of traditional Friday prayer attire that I was familiar with seeing Indian and Pakistani men wear to the Friday prayer in the UAE. I looked toward the doctor and asked if the muezzin would be willing to recite the adhan, and the muezzin looked at me and then looked at the doctor. He said something about how the adhan should not be recited off of the proper timings. The muezzin then excused himself to prepare for the adhan. I thanked him and placed my hand to my heart, a common greeting in India particularly between men and women who are not family.

I told the doctor I would head over to the other side of the circle to record the adhan, and I thanked him. The adhan sounded within ten minutes of the time that the video shop owner and his wife said it would. I knew the adhan was about to begin when I heard a click sound through the mosque loudspeaker. I had learned to listen carefully for this sound, often the sound of the on-off switch on the microphone being flicked from one position to the other, as it usually preceded the adhan by only seconds. My recorder was on, and I braced myself to minimize any handling noise, and to try and avoid noisy car horns for the next two to three minutes. The Maghreb Adhan sounded just before the sun fell, and the muezzin's voice was a beautiful complement to the soundscape of the traffic circle.

Bangalore, India, 2010   137

Figure 20.1   Masjid E Noor, Bangalore, India.

By the time I switched my recorder off and looked around, the lights of the mosque had been switched on to greet the night, and the minarets were glowing green. I hailed an auto-rickshaw in the traffic circle and made my way back to the Rajajinagar House. "Boss, Navrang Theater, malum hain?" [Do you know the Navrang Theater?] He moved his head back and forth and up and down in recognition. "Acha, challo" [Let's go], I said. And we were off (figure 20.1 and recording 21).

Recording #21   Masjid E Noor, Bangalore, India—Maghrib Adhan.

Chapter 21

Stockholm, Sweden, 2017

In late November of 2017 I flew into Stockholm, Sweden for one day on my way to a conference at Linköping University, located two hours southwest of the city by train. The conference, "Thinking through the Digital in Literature," was a gathering of thirty-five to forty writers, artists, and academics all interested in the relationship between literature and the digital. I prepared a talk for the conference about a hybrid media composition that I had created in response to Gertrude Stein's 1925 essay, *Composition as Explanation*. I spoke about the process of envisioning and creating the composition, the rationale behind why it was created, and the pedagogical as well as research-related implications of the piece for my own practice and teaching within the arts in higher education. My presentation consisted of twenty minutes of me introducing the piece, and an additional ten minutes of playing the composition for the audience. The piece, *Composition as Exploration*, a clear play on Stein's essay title, was presented in a video format. The piece combines animation, text, and recorded real-time sonic performance where I attempted to shift the meaning of the essay through the essay's form, by reproducing the essay's form through the live playing of a series of oscillators controlling parameters including pitch, tempo, and amplitude. The resulting product, as you might imagine, is somewhat experimental, making it the perfect piece for a conference that explores the digital and literature.

I had read an article in advance of my trip to Sweden. The article was from 2013 and marked a key decision made by the Swedish government to allow the Fittja Grand Mosque, in the suburbs of Stockholm, to sound the adhan for the Friday Jumu'ah Prayer. I read several articles about the decision in an attempt to find out a few key things. The first was whether or not the adhan was amplified at prayer times outside of the Friday Jumu'ah prayer, and the second was whether or not other Swedish mosques were given the same permission. Namely, I was interested in recording the adhan at the Stockholm Grand Mosque or as it is called in Swedish, the Islamiska Förbundet Stockholms Moské, which was a twenty-five-minute walk from where I was staying.

After navigating the bus ride from the airport and trying to follow a screen-grab of a map, as I didn't have a Swedish SIM card or international reception on my phone, I finally arrived at my Airbnb. Sofia, the owner, met me on the main street and showed me around the lovely 500-year-old apartment, pointing out how things worked and where I could return the key when I departed the following day. I asked Sofia if I was likely to hear the call to prayer sound at the Central Stockholm Mosque. She looked at me, head cocked to the side, a little unsure about how to answer me. I explained that I conduct research on the adhan, and whenever I visit a new place I try to visit a local mosque and record the call to prayer. Sofia said she was unsure and couldn't recall ever hearing the call to prayer. She did mention that it might be illegal, and she referenced the government decision to allow prayers at the Fittja mosque, suggesting I visit there instead.

Once Sofia left, I switched on the mobile Wi-Fi router at the Airbnb and searched for the prayer times in Stockholm. I had not yet recorded the adhan in a place that had very few hours of daylight and I was curious how the prayer times would be impacted by the extremely short days. Given that the prayer times are set based on the rising and setting of the sun, I figured that all of the prayer times might be highly condensed into a few hours of the day. My favorite adhan timing website islamicfinder.org said the Stockholm Isha'a prayer be at 5:26 pm. It was only 12:30 pm and I was exhausted from the overnight flight. I made a plan to settle in a bit, take a nap and shower, and head off to the Stockholm Grand Mosque later on.

The mosque is in a nondescript building on a quiet dark street in Stockholm. What appears to be the main entrance, a row of four simple wooden doors on the most well-lit end of the building, had a white paper sign taped up that said go around to back. Around the back, there was another identical set of four wooden doors on a very dark street abutting a small park that one can enter by going up a concrete staircase of ten steps. I grabbed the handle of one of the four doors to pull it open. It was much heavier than expected. The door opened into a glass-enclosed entryway. Through an open single glass door was an atrium with a chandelier hanging and green tiles lining the walls. There was a semicircular wooden desk directly across from the glass door that reminded me of the reception desk at the Jewish Community Center in the town where I grew up on Long Island. I greeted the man in the skullcap behind the desk, "As-salām alaykum." "Wa alaykum as-salām," he replied.

I explain I am an academic, conducting a research project on the adhan at mosques around the world. I also mention that I recently recorded the adhan in Iceland, and I ask if it would be okay if I record the adhan at their mosque. The man behind the desk gestures toward a pamphlet housed in a pamphlet holder sitting on the semicircular desk. I look at the pamphlet, which has the adhan times for September through December printed inside. I flip to November 28th, and see that the last adhan of the day, the Isha'a Adhan, is meant to be at 16:26 or 4:26 pm. I looked down at my watch, it was 5:10 pm. I had speed-walked from my accommodation to the mosque in order to make it in time for the 5:26 pm adhan, the time Islamic Finder listed. My heart dropped a bit with disappointment. This was not the first time I had arrived at a mosque to find out that my research had revealed prayer times different from the actual times that were recited. I was disappointed as I was only in Stockholm for one day, meaning I was going to miss recording the adhan altogether.

"6:00 pm," he said. "The adhan will be at 6:00 pm."
"Oh," I said, with relief in my voice.
"Will the adhan sound inside the prayer room and outside the mosque?"
   I asked the man with the skullcap.
"Only inside," he said.

The man looked at me and then gestured to the left. He walked out from behind the semicircular desk and into the mosque shop. I followed him. The mosque shop appeared to sell prayer rugs, books and skull caps among other things. He exchanged a few words with the man behind the shop counter who was folding garments. The man with the skullcap looked back over at me and asked if I had a phone I would record on. "Yes, I have a phone and an audio recorder."
   The two men discussed further. Then the man with the skullcap told me that it was okay with the muezzin, the man he had been speaking with behind the shop counter, if I recorded him reciting the adhan. I turned toward the muezzin and said shukran and then said the same to the man with the skullcap. I walked out of the shop and back toward the welcome desk.
   I was wearing a black hat because of the cold winter weather in Stockholm. The hat did cover all of my hair like a hijab or headscarf would, but it wasn't the traditional attire for a woman to enter the prayer room of a mosque. I turned back toward the man with the skull cap to ask if it would be okay if I wore my hat inside the prayer room, and if not, that I was happy to go into the shop to buy a headscarf.

"No, no it is okay with the hat," he responded. "Do you know where the
   prayer room is located?"
"Yes," I replied. "It is around the corner and up the stairs."

He nodded, and I turned to head for the ladies' prayer room entrance, which was just to the left through a threshold in the wall. There was another woman sitting on a chair in the shoe area, replacing her shoes and preparing to go back out into the cold. I sat on the small red wooden bench up against the wall that faced the ladies' entry doors, and removed my boots and placed them into the shoe cubby. The woman and I greeted each other and smiled. I continued up the staircase that was visible from the shoe rack alcove, removing my outer layers one by one as I climbed the stairs. First, my scarf came off and I placed it and my gloves into my jacket pocket. Then I removed my jacket, all the while careful not to remove my hat. When I reached the top of the stairs I did a quick check to ensure my hair was entirely tucked into the hat.

At the top of the stairs was a bathroom for ablution, a small hallway with several doors, and to the right a semicircular balcony that overlooked the reception area with a fantastic view of the chandelier. There was a six-foot-tall privacy barrier made of wooden lattice which wrapped around the edge of the semi-circular balcony, affording women their privacy from the male visitors who would enter through the main door below as I had. There were children running and playing about in the ladies' prayer room, which was the entire upstairs of the mosque. I saw a small children's room that looked like a family-style prayer room similar in design to the main prayer room, a carpeted open space, but where children were encouraged to run and play.

I wandered down the small narrow hallway, passing a few offices, the bathrooms and what smelled like a kitchen as I headed toward the ladies' prayer room. I entered the prayer room somewhat apprehensive. I felt out of place entering unaccompanied by a member of the community, and a bit self-conscious about the choice to wear my black hat in lieu of a more traditional head covering. The room was large and dark due to there being no sun, with somewhat low ceilings. I was immediately struck by the large green carpet that covered the floor, which included woven-in prayer designation lines that served as a guide for prayer goers to know where to line up.

The ladies' prayer room overlooked the main prayer room below for men, from where the muezzin would recite the adhan and the imam would give the sermon and lead prayers. There was a similar privacy screen around the perimeter of the ladies' prayer room balcony, again creating privacy between the two prayer areas. The diamond-shaped holes in the wooden lattice were fairly large and allowed for good visual sightlines to the main prayer room and good sonic transmission from the amplification down below up to the balcony. There were bookshelves scattered throughout the ladies' prayer room filled with stunningly bound Qur'ans, few of which were the same. There appeared to be other texts on the shelves as well, all with solid color bindings and inscribed golden Arabic script which flowed across the covers and spines. There were chairs placed haphazardly throughout the room as though they are often moved from place to place, and there were simple metal coat racks, one on each side of the main entrance to the room, where people placed their outerwear before finding a space to pray. I removed a metal hanger from the coat rack, as to not make too much noise, and placed my heavy gray Carhartt jacket on the hanger with scarf and gloves protruding from the unzipped side pockets. I gently placed the hanger back on the rack.

There was one woman in the prayer room when I first entered. She was sitting on the floor checking her phone, while her bags were perched on a chair next to her as though she was waiting for something. I greeted her.

"As-salām alaykum."

The woman replied in kind, with a common response to this greeting, peace be upon you also.

"Wa alaykum as-salām."

I continued past the woman and headed toward the back of the long prayer room, in an attempt to ascertain from where the muezzin would recite the adhan. I wanted to locate myself near to the lattice divider on the side of the room closest to the mihrab, the ornamental indentation in the wall that faces the direction of Mecca, as this is where the muezzin stands to recite the adhan.

Another woman entered the prayer room in a black abaya and headscarf. She walked into the small square part of the room, just next to the coat racks, faced the same direction as the mihrab and began the salah, the physical, spiritual, and mental act of worship. I had seen many people perform the salah and had even seen signs in my father's family mosque, which visually illustrated the steps for correctly performing the salah and wudu, the ritual washing before prayer. The salah fascinated me as a ritual gestural act, which all Muslims perform in the same way. When I was in a mosque, I found myself wanting to look at a woman performing salah, to watch her movement and gesture, to try and remember the order, and follow along in my mind. I found the salah completely mesmerizing, and at the same time, confusing and unfamiliar. And I also didn't want to watch her perform salah, because it felt like an invasion of her private space during worship, and because it felt strange for me to be in her place of worship as a guest, staring at her praying.

This was one of those confusing moments while conducting ethnographic research as an artist. It is that moment when one's internal barometer for what is ethical throws up a red flag. This moment occurred at the Stockholm Grand Mosque when I remembered there is a difference between being a visitor to a mosque and being a participant observer or an artist with a critical eye toward gesture, color, and movement. I wanted to watch the woman perform salah in part, because I am interested in knowing how to perform it, and yet I am aware that performing the physical movements or actions is not the same as performing the salah, which is as much a spiritual and devotional act as it is a series of gestures where one bows, kneels, and prostrates. I watched the woman pray from behind for a short while, observing her actions and the ritualistic nature of them, and then I continued on to prepare to record.

The men's or main prayer room was a beautiful large open space, with a similar green carpet to that in the ladies' prayer room, adorned with large hanging chandeliers and a multi archway threshold dividing the front and back spaces of the room. The mihrab (the alcove facing Mecca) and minbar (the pulpit from where the imam speaks) were housed in a decorative area at the front of the room. I looked up at the ceiling, which was covered in tiles of multiple shades of green. There were large metal beams, painted green, running across the width of the space as though they were structurally holding up the room. I wondered if perhaps this building had at one time housed an indoor swimming pool.

I sat down next to the wooden lattice divider on the right side of the balcony, which overlooked the mihrab. There was a chair where I could sit while I waited fifteen minutes for the recitation of the adhan. I took the audio recorder out of my bag, turned it on, and adjusted the microphone levels based on the decibel meter reading of the ambient noises of the space, chatter, room tone, heating, and so on. I placed the earbuds in my ears and monitored the sound coming through the recorder. I experimented with the best placement for the audio recorder, ideally one where the built-in XY microphones could stick through the diamond-shaped hole in the lattice's cross thatch. More women entered the prayer room as the adhan time approached. I have found that in many mosques I have visited, the adhan is truly a call to the mosque, around which time the mosque fills with worshippers.

I had my eye on the mihrab thinking that the muezzin would be standing there to recite the adhan. I was so focused on the mihrab that I missed the muezzin making his way, and instead heard the adhan before seeing the muezzin. This is one of many times that my listening skills were paramount to recording in the field. I began this research process prizing my vision as the default sense to guide my understanding of an environment, but quickly learned that in fact when focusing on sound and recording, trusting my listening skills and honing my listening sense proved paramount. The adhan was beautifully recited and was different from any other I had heard. It did, in some ways, have some similar resonances and tonal qualities to the adhan I

Figure 21.1   Islamiska Förbundet Stockholms Moské, Stockholm, Sweden.

had recorded in Reykjavik. Immediately after the recitation concluded, the imam who was seated in the minbar began speaking into the microphones mounted to the side railing. At this point, I quietly packed up the audio recorder and after five minutes or so made my way to the coat rack, where I collected my belongings and headed down the stairs. I put my boots back on, zipped up my coat, put on my scarf and gloves, and ventured out of the ladies' prayer room side door onto the dark city street (figure 21.1 and recording 22).

Recording #22   Islamiska Förbundet Stockholms Moské, Stockholm, Sweden.

Chapter 22

Ethnography and the Sonic Frame

Numerous composers from the early and mid-twentieth century, including Luigi Russolo, Edgard Varése, and later Jacques Attali, were in agreement that noise was an important element of a composition, as well as an indicator of society. In the first chapter of his book, *Noise: The Political Economy of Music*, Attali wrote "music, the organization of noise is one such form. It reflects the manufacture of society; it constitutes the audible waveband of the vibrations and signs that make up society." Attali's book is written in part, as he says, to "not only theorize about music, but to theorize through music."[1] In a related way, this book not only is interested in writing and by extension theorizing about sound, specifically recordings of the call to prayer, but also offers as its method theorizing through recorded sound. By listening to the recordings of the adhan on the soundmap, we are listening as much to the recitation of the adhan (often already transformed from live to amplified), as we are to the audible attributes of each community—those things that make up the social structure of each place.

The geographically based ethnographic case studies in this book are based largely on details embedded in the supplementary sounds captured in the field recordings from each community. The words on these pages are translations through memory of these first-encounter experiences, the details of which have been facilitated by listening back to the field recordings made in each place. This is my method for analyzing the field recordings I have collected, and for writing up these case studies of ethnographic research. I rely on field recordings to inform my memory as they capture a sonic snapshot that is more complete than what I can recall from memory alone, and to serve as the basis for the imagery, language, and detail that I include in each chapter of this book.

The field recordings I have made for this project span anywhere from ten minutes to two hours. The recitations of the adhan that I have recorded have taken between forty-five seconds and five-and-a-half minutes to be recited, depending on the style and speed of the recitation. The remaining time on each field recording includes sounds of the environment, conversations, and exchanges with people in the community. They contain sonic information that evokes feelings from a given moment and information that triggers bodily sense-based memories, details, and inner thoughts, which remind me of how I navigated the encounter both inwardly and outwardly. These protracted recordings are filed into a folder on my computer with the name of the mosque and categorized by country. They live there alongside the extracted recordings of the adhan, which have been posted to the soundmap along with photographs of the mosques.

Critical to ethnographic research is the relationship the researcher has to the people and communities they research and their reflexive orientation to themselves. It is worth noting that while I do believe a field recording can capture a more complete snapshot of a given moment than my memory, it is important to state that the snapshot I record is particular to my orientation to the community and will sound different from the snapshot someone else records. What a recording captures is directly tied to the type of comfort, access, and relationship the recordist has to the people and community they are in.

Take as an example the soundmap recording of the adhan from the King Hussein Mosque in Amman, Jordan. You might notice that the recording sounds like it is made in a noisy outdoor area—it was recorded from the square outside the mosque—and that the footsteps and chatter of passersby feel more prominent than the adhan. These sounds sonically place the recordist outside the mosque among the crowds of visitors and tourists, which is exactly representative of the vantage point I brought to that particular recording. I was not very comfortable going inside of mosques at the beginning of this project, when I made the recording at the King Hussein Mosque, and had difficulty identifying when and where it was appropriate for me to enter. I was not comfortable with how to act and conduct myself inside the mosque,

Recording #23 King Hussein Mosque, Amman, Jordan.

and I was very uncertain of how to communicate my motivations for being there. This lack of comfort directly impacted all of the initial recordings I made for the soundmap, and if you listen for it you will notice that early on in the project many of my recordings were made outside of mosques because of this discomfort about going inside (recording 23).

As the project has progressed, I have become more comfortable with entering mosques. This has been the result of educating myself, asking questions, learning about appropriate conduct inside mosques, about the salah prayers, and by studying Arabic so I can read things in Arabic, communicate basic greetings, and properly pronounce relevant words and phrases. As the project and my comfort going inside mosques progressed, the recordings I made were more often taken from inside the women's prayer area of the mosque. If you listen carefully, you might notice some of the subtleties unique to a recording made in a space for women and children. These include the absence of male voices other than the muezzins and imams, the voices of women, sometimes the playful shrill of children and always their chatter, all in a space that is typically smaller and more enclosed than the main prayer room. All of this is revealed in the sonic resonance of the recording.

Through the process of developing the soundmap of the adhan, I have had a number of contributors send recordings they have made within their own communities, and without fail these recordings capture a uniquely different sonic snapshot of a place, one where the recordist is clearly a part of the community they are recording. These recordings leave me with a more intimate feeling than the experience I have when listening to those I have made. In these recordings, what is most clear is that the act of recording the adhan was not the primary reason for being at the mosque. While the quality of the recording is not always ideal with handling noise and movement often audible, there is something else that comes through, which I would call a sense of familiarity with the environment. For me as a listener, this more familiar orientation of the recordist to a community creates a sense of proximity, access, and sometimes even intimacy. A friend and former colleague, Omer Ahmed, has made many contributions to the soundmap through the years, and below he reflects on his own orientation to the adhan and interest in recording the call to prayer.

AN INSIDER PERSPECTIVE BY OMER "KASHMIR" AHMED

For as long as I can remember, I have always been fascinated by the various styles of *adhan* from all over the world. The first time I fell in love with it was in 2009. I witnessed the collective intoning of the *adhan* by six muezzins, a unique practice of the centuries-old Jami' Umawi (the Umayyad Mosque) located near Souk al-Hamidiyah in the old city of Damascus. My love affair with the *adhan* was re-ignited years later in Abu Dhabi when Diana shared her plans on the then emerging *adhan* project. As immaterial as it may have been, I knew I had to play my part in ensuring that this remarkable initiative reached its full potential.

Muslims believe that it is *sunnah* to give *adhan* in a newborn baby's right ear and *iqamah* in their left ear. This heralds the beginning of a lifetime of conversation with the muezzin. Similarly, my trivial contribution to this nonpareil project has had a profound impact on me, as it has allowed me to enjoy innumerable provoking conversations with many muezzin over *qahwa* (coffee) and *tamar* (dates). In some cases, these discussions led to the beginning of new relationships, emotional recitations of the Qur'an, melodious hymnodies, and remembrance and commemoration of Allah in the form of *dhikr*. I have come to appreciate the different styles of *adhan* and the factors influencing them, such as prophetic tradition, culture, and the distinctive identity and charisma of the muezzin himself.

My experience recording the *adhan* across the globe has been nothing short of unique and memorable. Each *masjid* has a story to tell. However,

Figure 22.1 Al-Masjid An-Nabawi, Medina, Kingdom of Saudi Arabia. *Source:* Image courtesy of Omer "Kashmir" Ahmed.

Recording #24 Al-Masjid An-Nabawi, Medina, Kingdom of Saudi Arabia—Isha'a Adhan. Recorded by Omer "Kashmir" Ahmed.

my visit to the breathtaking *Al-Masjid An-Nabawi* (the Prophet's Mosque) in Medina is hard to describe in words. The recording captures the mosque's foundations laid by the Prophet (PBUH), Umar and Uthman's expansion of the mosque, and the endless restorations and extensions by many empires including the Turkish Ottomans. While the colossal building is equipped with loudspeakers that helps transmit the *adhan* all around the mosque, radiating sound on to the surrounding streets, getting that perfect mix of sound was crucial. My aim was to encapsulate the clarity of the muezzin, while capturing the historic character of the building, complemented by the sounds of the worshippers. I tested various locations before I settled for the ideal one. I showed up early for *salah* that day, so I could weave through a dense congregation of worshippers to be as close to the muezzin as possible.

I tested the recording device several times to avoid any misadventures and kept an eye out for signs of the start of the *adhan*, so I could capture it in its entirety. At last, all I had to do was press record and watch the magic unfold. I am pleased to say that Diana's *adhan* project has given my conversations with the muezzin a new dimension. (figure 22.1 and recording 24)

ETHNOGRAPHIC POSITIONALITY

Of the many definitions of ethnography out there, Sarah Pink's remains the one I am most partial to because of its recognition of the complexity and ever-changing nature of ethnographic research in a contemporary world. In 2016, Pink et al. published a definition of digital ethnography that feels germane to my research:

> "An approach to doing ethnography in a contemporary world . . . [it] also explores the consequences of the presence of digital media in shaping the techniques and processes through which we practice ethnography, and accounts for

how the digital, methodological, practical and theoretical dimensions of ethnographic research are increasingly intertwined."[2]

I am as concerned with the social world I study as I am with the digital tools I use for collecting and disseminating recordings, and the practical work that comes out of my research. This definition of digital ethnography inspires me to look at the edges of my intertwined scholarly and creative practice, and to see where they blur and where there may be the creation of new knowledge that exists at the nexus of the practical and theoretical.

As an ethnographer using field recordings, my practice relies on developing, sometimes very quickly, relationships with members of the communities I visit in order to gain access and permission to record in the community. I have found that this is a more complicated task than gaining permission to have a conversation, but an easier task than trying to photograph a person or conduct a video interview of them. Sometimes, I cannot gain explicit permission to record because there is no one to ask, or I make my intentions known and ask for permission but to someone other than the person whose voice I am recording. Other times, I simply record sounds from outside a mosque, like the recording of the Salah Al-Deens Mosque near Mt. Nebo in Jordan, where at times several recitations can be heard simultaneously (figure 22.2 and recording 25).

Figure 22.2 Salah Al-Deens Mosque Near Mt. Nebo, Jordan.

Recording #25   Salah Al-Deens Mosque near Mt. Nebo, Jordan—Dhuhr Adhan.

These recitations of the adhan in the public listening domain, outside of mosques, become sonic elements of the public soundscape. In this way, the nature of sound is different from the visual. Sound is all around us. It travels and reflects. Sometimes, depending on the wind or the material surfaces on streets, buildings, and in nature, a sound can be thrown through the air or bounce off one spot and present itself in another.

I record many sounds, including voices of people that I don't intend to, and sometimes don't realize I am capturing at that moment. Should I ask for permission to record someone who is passing by on the street talking loudly, or the children screaming as they run through the prayer room while my equipment is in record mode? Realistically, there are many moments where I simply can't get permission for the many sounds that end up in my field recordings. It is the constructed sonic vantage point made from these unintended recorded sounds, together with those that were the focus of the recording, that allows me to write in the depth I do about these encounters in this book and that creates the sonic contexts you the listeners hear.

My task in conducting research of a particular Muslim community, therefore, becomes a task of asking for permission when I can, speaking to community members when I can, documenting the place and surroundings, and collecting field recordings that I will later analyze. These are the initial steps of my field recording method, and many of the decisions I make about the collection and analysis of my research are connected to these initial decisions. As I mentioned, the method I use for analyzing my data includes retrospectively listening to the unedited field recordings and writing up my notes through the process of memory recall, triggered by the sonic details of the recordings. I have found this practice to help inform and shape my understanding of the place where I was conducting research, from a birds-eye view, allowing me to see the unfolding of the research more clearly through the data. Perhaps, a more accurate way to represent this practice would be to call it a retrospective sonic orientation to a particular encounter, whereby immersing myself in the field recording gives me access to the experiences and memories of conducting the research, with the added bonus of being able to also focus on the collected sonic data, allowing me to synthesize my memory with the sonic information captured in the field recordings. This allows me a deeper dive into my field research than memory or field notes alone, and importantly allows me to consider data I was not focused on when conducting the research. This is because the microphone picks up everything in its field, not simply those things I am focused on at the time of recording.

My positionality or how I fit within the cultural and social framework of the places I visit, impacts how I am perceived, how my actions are understood, and how I approach the recordings I make. When I conduct research outside of a familiar cultural framework, the visual and sonic references of that place don't often mean what I think they do. I need to learn new references in order to understand a new cultural context. For example, the first time I traveled to Delhi, I was surprised by how often people honked their horns while driving. It seemed that the drivers were impatient and short-tempered, honking at the drop of a hat. After a month living in Delhi, I had many more experiences or data of being in the honking traffic. This included as a passenger in an auto-rickshaw, on a motorcycle on local roads, in a car on the highway at night alongside lorries with the words, HONK WHEN PASSING painted on the back door, as a passenger on a bus that while climbing mountain passes seemed to incessantly honk, and as a pedestrian witnessing the honking from outside it all.

What I realized after having these varied experiences over a period of time, is that in India horns are used to signal many things and are not simply a warning signal or aggressive gesture, which is how they are used in New York where I grew up. Honking is used to communicate 'I'm passing you' as in the case with cars passing trucks on the highways at night, or 'I am coming up on your right don't veer out of your lane,' another common communication on the highway. Honking is used sometimes along with hand gestures to communicate, 'you go ahead,' or 'pull over,' and sometimes to simply present one's self as is the case with buses that honk often to signal their presence to potential passengers as they drive past. Honking is also a communication technique used by motorcyclists when they are riding on the sidewalk and want to warn pedestrians they are coming, or whenever any driver thinks they may be in another driver's blind spot, or to get the attention of a driver who you think may be distracted. As a new listener to Delhi honking, it's no wonder I got it all wrong. It would have been impossible for me to apply my New York understanding of honking as a sonic symbol or cue, to accurately interpret what someone meant while honking in Delhi. Even when one does know the context, the multitude of meanings can make it difficult to make sense of road honking, but at least the honking can be contextualized within a Delhi framework.

I now consider as my starting point that it takes time to make sense of new cultural contexts, and apply this thinking to how I might be perceived within the contexts where I record. I imagine how someone unfamiliar with audio recording equipment might make sense of me holding out a microphone with a large fuzzy windscreen on it. I imagine that a person's reference for understanding the optics of the windscreen-covered microphone would be tied to other similar things they have seen before. Also, their visual reference would include and be inextricably linked to the person holding the microphone—what that person looks like and where they are from. More than a handful of times, I have had people wonder whether or not the microphone I was carrying was a weapon, in particular some form of a gun. And every time this happened, I was grateful that I was not wearing any form of military or combat attire, but instead a headscarf, and that as a woman in the communities where I record, most people would not assume that I was in fact holding a weapon. However, I also walk into every recording situation aware that a shotgun microphone, aptly named, can and has been mistaken for a gun, and so I proceed cautiously and with the expectation that someone in eyeshot of me might not be sure what I am holding or that it may be visually understood as a weapon.

As a result, I do not record in interior religious spaces with fuzzy windscreens or large microphones, as I have found that the fuzzy cover, more than anything else, gives off a different visual cue than I realize or intend. I prefer to record with a small form factor digital audio recorder with onboard microphones, as this allows me to hold the device like a large mobile phone or mp3 player, set it up with a simple pair of high-quality earbuds, and then leave the device either on the floor out of my hands, or seated in a bag that I have brought. I can still adjust levels and monitor the recording as needed. But by removing the device from my hands, and in some cases from public view, I notice that I can be in the space and record without creating a spectacle with the equipment.

I have made many adjustments to my recording practice as a result of learning that my presence augments the recordings I make. As I have argued earlier in this chapter when talking about positionality, my very presence in a space I am not usually in, does affect the ethos of the place during my visit for the simple reason that unlike most other women in the ladies prayer rooms I visit, I am not there to pray but rather to record.

Chapter 23

Singapore, 2014

It's funny how time constraints can be a motivator. I find that if I am visiting somewhere for a week, it is almost a given that I will make a point of visiting a local mosque and recording the call to prayer. However, I seem to be less dogmatic about recording in the places where I live, probably because there is no rush. It's easy to fall back on the common trope of procrastination and think I will do it another day. While I lived in Singapore I would pass mosques all over the city, but never stopped with a recorder in hand at prayer time ready to record.

Adjacent to the apartment complex where I lived in Clementi—a western suburban part of Singapore where the National University of Singapore is located—there is a mosque up on a hill. I passed this mosque and the stairs leading up to it, countless times while walking to the bus or on a bike ride. After living in Singapore for several months I decided it was time to take out my audio recorder and visit the mosque, Masjid Tentera Diraja. Being an equatorial country, Singapore is known for its humidity. On most days, even a walk to the bus stop results in a light full body sweat. I walked to the mosque and stood down at sidewalk level looking up. I took a few photographs and waited for the adhan to sound. I waited for roughly thirty minutes but didn't see anyone walk in or out of the mosque, and I didn't hear the adhan sound.

I decided I would try visiting another local mosque to see if the adhan would sound there. Near the post office, a thirty-minute walk away from Masjid Tentera Diraja, there is another small mosque embedded in a neighborhood. I planned to visit the mosque another day, preferably one with a slight breeze so I could ride my bike there. I grabbed my audio recorder, headphones, and bottle of water, and jumped onto my bike. The neighborhood near the post office has small streets, large trees that hang over the streets, and each home has its own driveway; this is posh for Singapore where the majority of the population live in Housing and Development Board flats (HDBs), or what I grew up thinking of as apartment towers. I set off down an interior winding road just off the main street, which felt hidden and private. At the bottom of a hill the road hooked to the left and on a grassy patch to the side of the hook was a small green mosque that blended in with the trees planted throughout the neighborhood.

There was a small green dome on the top of the mosque, and the awning was a deep green. I could see a main door to the mosque and to the left of it, an open-air overhang where it looked like community events may be held. There was a man underneath the overhang cleaning off lunch dishes. His scooter was parked just off to the side, and it didn't take long before he spotted me.

"Hello," I said, placing my hand to my chest. He nodded. The man had dark brown skin and looked East Asian. I thought he might be Malay Singaporean, as many are Muslims, whereas many Indian Singaporeans are often Hindu, and Chinese Singaporeans either Christian or Buddhist. He continued about his business cleaning up outside. I moved my way around the open outdoor area, careful to not step foot inside. I loitered for another five minutes, and when the man looked up from what he was doing, I decided I would try to engage him again. "Hello Sir. What time is the adhan?" He looked at me. He looked at his watch. He informed me it was coming, soon it would be prayer time. Then the harder part, trying to figure out whether or not the adhan would sound at the mosque. I asked, "does the adhan sound?" He looked at me clearly puzzled at what I was saying. "The adhan," I said, "Adhan." "Adhan?" He replied. "Yes," I moved my head forward and smiled. He said, "No no no adhan." "Where?" I asked. He said, "Sultan Mosque."

I did some enquiring and learned that in Singapore, there are many rules about religious sounds in public spaces. As it turned out, the Sultan Mosque on Arab Street was one of the few mosques in the city that was allowed to sound the adhan. That was what the man was trying to tell me, that I had to go to the Sultan Mosque.

Arab Street was much further from where I was staying than the thirty-minute walk to the green mosque near the post office. As a result, it was a few weeks after my first attempt at recording the adhan when I finally made my way to Arab Street. Arab Street is an area comprised of a number of streets, which more or less dead ends into the very prominent-looking Sultan Mosque. Historically, this part of Singapore was predominantly home to Muslim families. There are a good number of restaurants and shops that sell Arab-style clothing. This is the part of Singapore where one can find cuisine from Lebanon, Turkey, Morocco, and beyond. I haven't seen any shisha shops in the area, though I imagine they exist. Arab Street also hosts a fun street market on weekends, where sellers, many from the Muslim community of Singapore, sell their wares including clothes, home goods, and books. Just outside the cozy somewhat touristy clustering of streets, is an outer circle of streets most of which sell more practical items for the Muslim community, including women's clothing, abayas, men's kurta pajama–style clothing, prayer rugs, and the like.

My first visit to Arab Street was great. To my surprise, I spent most of the trip traveling up and down the main strip with my friend, exploring the interesting coffee shops, bars, and Tibetan clothing stores nestled into the street-level storefronts in the old Chinese shophouses. Arab Street also offers a vibrant nightlife facilitated by the small pedestrian-only streets. There are a number of late-night music venues on the upper floors, and some bars that slide open their doors and windows to break the barrier between street and shop, where they set up small stages facing outward toward patrons who sit around tables erected in the middle of the road.

As the sun moved lower in the sky, I made my way to Masjid Sultan, a large beautiful mosque that towers over the whole of the Arab Street area with its imposing stature. Just outside the front of the mosque, there is a message board with information about community events, and prayer times. And just beyond, there are several benches under some trees for taking a rest. This is where I planted myself and my audio recorder, waiting. I was hopeful but not certain that the adhan would sound from this mosque, given my initial experience, and the fact that there weren't many people around. A man rode up to the mosque on his scooter, got off, locked the scooter and walked inside the mosque. Then another man rode up and did the same thing, and then another. They all locked their bikes up against the black iron gate between the mosque and the road and walked inside a small door off to the side of the mosque.

I pulled out my audio recorder and headphones and started making some test recordings from the bench. Adjusting levels and placing the windscreen on the microphones, I spent 15 minutes listening to the sounds of Arab Street with my eyes closed, only through the headphones on my ears. Allowing the sound recorder to mediate the experience actually made me feel more connected to the environment than the half day I had spent walking around it. I think, at the time, there was something about the grandeur of the exterior of the Sultan Mosque and the gate that surrounded it, which made me feel disconnected. Also, this was earlier on in both my recording practice and my ethnographic research, and I was shy and uncertain of how to engage with this particular community that I knew little about. As a result, during this visit, I didn't end up speaking to anyone from the mosque community. I didn't go up to the mosque, look for the office or the imam and ask if I could record the prayer, or if I they would allow me to enter the women's prayer room. This experience of recording was done entirely from the bench under the tree across from the mosque, and the experience became about me and my orientation to the process of trying to track down the call to prayer.

I heard the familiar click of the amplification system switching on, and then it started; a very raw and beautiful adhan, unlike any I had heard before. The muezzin's recitation came blasting through the speakers, sounding like the amplification system might explode. The adhan sounded as though it was resonating through a mountain village, and I was hearing it from a great distance. While the speakers seemed, both visually and sonically, that they were of a high quality, unlike some of the tinny or distorted sounding systems I had heard through the years, the adhan had an echo or reverb effect added to it. I imagine this reverb effect was added as a part of the analog audio chain. There was a second distinctive quality to the amplified recitation. It was coming out of the speaker too hot, meaning that the gain structure of the microphone was too high, and the resulting amplified sound had high-end feedback. The playback sounded as though it was pushing against the limitations of the speaker.

The muezzin utilized a recitation style that I was partially familiar with in that his style was full of vocal flourishings, but very unfamiliar in the key and

Figure 23.1 Masjid Sultan, Singapore.

Singapore, 2014

Recording #26   Masjid Sultan, Singapore.

flourishing decisions he made. I wondered where the muezzin was from and how this recitation style had been cultivated.

Singapore is a relatively young country, just over fifty-five years old, with an interesting history. In 1963, Malaysia was formed comprising the Federation of Malaya, Singapore, Sarawak, and North Borneo (now Sabah), and less than two years later in 1965, Singapore left Malaysia and became an independent sovereign nation. Singapore is comprised of three main ethnic groups who make up its citizenry: the Chinese majority who are primarily Christian though there is a large number of Buddhists, the Malays who are primarily Muslims, and the Tamil Indians who are primarily Hindu. As a result, the Muslim community in Singapore is largely comprised of Singaporean Malays. I wondered if the muezzin was Malay, or if perhaps he studied or was from outside of Singapore. I was curious about the recitation style but had no firsthand information from the community to help make sense of it. The next step would be to go back to the mosque to speak with someone about these questions in order to learn more about the place (figure 23.1 and recording 26).

It was now dark as the sun had set, and my friend and I weaved our way through the dark streets. We wandered through some small backstreets and found our way to the main road. These back alleys were where people parked their cars and put out trash for collection. I noticed a mannequin torso in a junk pile, and just beside it was a brown paper bag with two mannequin arms sticking out. There was a young couple making out just across the way, and I not so accidentally interrupted their private moment to ask if they thought the mannequin was someone's or if it was being thrown out. I didn't want to run the risk of stealing something from someone especially in Singapore, where I didn't know the local laws very well. They told me it was garbage. I picked up the mannequin torso, awkwardly wrapping my arms around her flat stomach, and my friend picked up the brown paper bag with her arms. We popped her in the trunk of the taxi and made our way back home.

Chapter 24

Madha, Oman, 2016

After completing a leave of absence in Singapore, I returned to Abu Dhabi where I would work one more year at NYU AD before moving on to new adventures. I had already given up my apartment in the tall residential tower in Khalidiya when I went to Singapore, and decided I would move into a small graduate student apartment at the university's new campus on Saadiyat Island. The studio was tiny but extremely well designed, furnished, and finished. There was a good-size bathroom in the apartment, a galley kitchen, and a double bed. The full length of the studio had floor-to-ceiling glass windows that looked away from the campus toward the water and Abu Dhabi City in the distance. The view was unobstructed, as no buildings had been erected between the university and the water at that time, making it the perfect spot for gazing out into the distance. I squished a small desk against the window that the galley kitchen dead-ended into. This was where I would spend most of that year writing my dissertation, and just next to the desk, I fit a tiny sitting area made up of two large multi-patterned wingback chairs I bought from a favorite imported furniture warehouse in Meena Port, and a small round table. It was the perfect little spot for writing, and while not ideal for hosting guests, the apartment suited me for that final year.

One day while writing, I received an email from my friend Robin, who I had shared many meals and conversations with while on leave in Singapore. He was on sabbatical and traveling around the world doing research for a new book he was writing on exclaves. He emailed to say he would be in Abu Dhabi for a conference and wanted to find time to catch up over a drink. He also hoped to visit Nahwa, an Emirati enclave, and Madha, an Omani exclave, and asked if I would like to accompany him on the excursion. It all sounded like a fun time to me.

Chapter 24

The last night of Robin's conference, I joined him and several of the organizers, also my friends and colleagues, out for drinks and dinner. Robin and I finalized our plan for that coming weekend, and I booked a car for us to take on our adventure. We met at 9:00 am on Saturday morning down in the university parking garage that connected all of the buildings underground. We traveled with our passports, in case there was a border-crossing checkpoint, some cash, and several large bottles of water. I brought an off-roading map book as a tool for navigation in case our mobile phone data stopped working partway through the trip, as usually happened in the UAE, rendering all map apps useless. We drove northeast from Abu Dhabi to Sharjah passing right through Dubai, then onward to the east on the interior road that cuts across the UAE from Sharjah on the strait of Hormuz, to Fujairah on the Gulf of Oman. Once we turned inland, the radio stations faded in and out of static, and boredom set in.

"I am very excited to visit Madha," Robin said, breaking the silence. "I'm not sure if I have mentioned this to you, but while Madha is an Omani exclave inside of the United Arab Emirates, Nahwa is an Emirati enclave inside of Madha."

To be honest, the whole thing was a bit confusing to me at first. Why would there be a small Omani territory completely landlocked by the UAE, when Oman shares a border with the UAE? And why is there then a tiny little Emirati territory inside of the Omani territory. Trying to make sense of the correlation between these places, I envisioned a bagel, where Nahwa was the hole.

As we drove along the interior highway that connects Sharjah to Fujairah, I was reminded of my summer visits to Fujairah's beachside resorts—an opportunity to escape a bit of the desert heat. The terrain changes when you drive across the UAE. The Strait of Hormuz side of the country is speckled with large cities and desert terrain, while the Gulf of Oman side is rocky and mountainous like Oman.

The road from Fujairah City to the town of Khor Fukkan in Sharjah, the closest town to the Omani exclave of Madha, is lined with large oil tanks that reminded me of short water towers. The smell of oil was heavy in the air on the main stretch of road, and through the traffic noise, one could hear the crashing of the waves from the Gulf of Oman visible out of the right side of the car. As we neared Khor Fukkan, we kept our eyes peeled for the road to Madha on the left. The main road into the exclave from this approach was two-sided with high sidewalks and tall lamp posts, making it distinctive from the surrounding area as though it was part of a film set. Off to the right-hand side of the entrance, there was a stone wall with a sign that read, Sultanate of Oman, with the Omani emblem, topped by two Omani flags that were blowing in the wind.

I drove through the stone wall entrance, the car flanked by tall glass-domed lamp posts lining the path. The lamp posts were jutting out of beds of soil in which there were many beautifully colored flowers planted. The reds, whites, yellows, and oranges reminded me of my trip to the Royal Palace in Muscat, the capital of Oman, where flowers like these were prominent along the palace roads. Robin and I looked at one another. We had found Madha. There wasn't a checkpoint or a guard's booth between the porous border of the UAE and the Omani exclave. We continued along the road and noticed small shops that had vinyl storefront signs stretched on metal frames reading, laundry, frozen foods, and haircuts.

We followed the one snaking road up and down, as we wove our way through mountains and over man-made bridges. The road was well paved as though it had recently been redone. Off the main road, there were smaller side streets made of packed sand and dirt that looked as though they may have, at one time, had a coating of tar or asphalt on top. The mountains on either side of these carved-out roads still had small pebbles at their base, tempting us to believe that perhaps the road we were driving down was made from the rock and rock dust removed from the mountain we were driving through. There weren't many vehicles on the road, though we did see a few homes, mostly single-story concrete with a goat or sheep roaming within a wire-fenced area.

We finally hit what looked like a small-town center with a mosque, a convenience store, and a school with a playground area for children that boasted six-foot-tall plastic palm trees. We entered the convenience store. There was a man sitting on a chair behind the counter toward the back of the store. The lights were switched off, and the shelves lining the long walls of the shop were sparsely stocked. There were a few canned items on one shelf, one container of cooking oil, and in the back a small cooler with beverages. The shelves on the right side of the shop were by comparison stocked with non-edible items including plastic water guns, clothes, and Emirati flags. I looked at Robin gesturing toward the flags. "We must be in Nahwa now—these are Emirati flags." Robin picked up two Emirati flags and handed them to the man in the back of the store along with a ten dirham note. He received change. We walked back out to the car and looked around. There wasn't a soul in site. There weren't any children on the playground equipment, there was no one else in or near the store, and no other cars passed us on the main road. A few buildings down there was a façade covered in a sun-weathered sign that looked like an old UAE shield at the top center, of two Emirati flags crisscrossing a tall palm tree. Beneath the palm tree in Arabic was the word Sharjah. Below the shield were the words Nahwa Power Station. We were definitely in Nahwa, the donut hole.

We hopped back in the car and continued driving until we crossed a wadi, riverbed, that was overflowing onto the road. We pulled over. There were people hanging out on the side of the wadi. An older couple had walked further into the wadi and were sitting under the shade of a palm tree on a big rock, with their feet in the water. There were children jumping up and down in the water and swimming in their clothes in the deeper areas. Robin and I enjoyed the shade while observing the micro-culture of the overflowing wadi. I stuck my foot into the water to see how it felt. The scene made me think of New York City fire hydrant culture, where someone would unscrew the cap on a fire hydrant so that water would come rushing out. All of the kids on the street would come out in their clothes or bathing suits, and dance around in the cool refreshing water on a hot day. The water would ultimately flood into the street and depending on the slope, move along the edge of the street toward a sewer grate.

Robin snapped a few photographs of the wadi, capturing the contrast of the oasis in such an arid climate, and walked back to the car. We drove on and came upon a small green park down a set of stairs from the road, which was built on the edge of a different wadi that was at that moment dried up. Inside the park, there were trees and a small gazebo for having picnics in, as well as children's playground toys, like a duck on a big spring that a child could sit on a bounce around. We noticed several women in abayas and children sitting and playing and chatting.

At this point, we had driven around the entirety of the main road and decided it was time to retrace our steps back in the opposite direction. As we drove back down the lamp post street, to the road that runs along the perimeter, I decided to U-turn in order to take a few photographs. I leaned out of the window to take a clear picture of the Sultanate of Oman sign. A large white Dodge pickup truck turned the corner from the entrance of the exclave onto the road where we were stopped. The truck was high off the ground, with dark tinted windows. The passenger side window lowered, and we could see a man in the driver's seat wearing reflective aviator sunglasses with a meticulously sculpted beard. He was wearing a white kandura, the national dress for men in the Gulf, and a red and white checked keffiyeh around his head. I rolled down Robin's window in kind and looked at the man with a half-smile.

"Hello, my friend, where are you from?" he asked.

Robin looked toward me, slightly uncomfortably.

"Hello," I said. "We are visiting from Abu Dhabi. We came to see Madha."

"I am from Madha," he said. "How do you find my place?"

"It is really nice," I responded. "We took a drive inside and we saw the Sadah Dam and we went to Nahwa as well."

"Okay and where are you from?" he asked.

"We are from the United States," I responded.

"I am Qamar from Madha."

"Are you married?" he asked.

"We are colleagues" . . . I paused wondering if that would answer his question. "We are friends," I responded.

"Okay so if you want you can come to my house," he offered. "I live very near to here just around the corner, I will show you."

I looked at Robin who had been pretty quiet. He didn't say anything. I lingered on his facial expression for a moment. "What do you want to do?"

"Well, what do you think?" He replied.

I turned back toward Qamar's car. "Yes, let's go to your house," I responded.

"Okay, you follow me," he said.

I rolled the window back up and put the car in to drive. Robin broke his silence.

"I am glad you handled that situation."

"That was a very typical exchange with an Emirati man, or possibly Omani, given where we are. He seems very nice."

Qamar's house was one storey and made of concrete. There weren't many windows, which was more than compensated for by the all-glass, tinted reflective extension that jutted out from the street side of the house almost all the way to where we parked the car beside the curb. Given the size of the prefabricated window room, I imagined it was Qamar's majlis. I had seen other similar majlis designs that were add ons to houses, an easy plug-and-play solution to creating a room that served a very important function in Arab culture, a room for entertaining guests and having important discussions.

Qamar pulled into his driveway and gestured for us to wait a minute, while he went inside a small concrete threshold at the back of the house. Moments later two children emerged from the same threshold and started unpacking groceries from the back of Qamar's vehicle. "These are my children," he said, while gesturing toward the children carrying grocery bags into the house. They looked curiously but shyly in our direction before dashing into the house with the bags.

I had learned all about majlises while living in Abu Dhabi. A friend's father was Emirati and inside his compound, which included several homes, he had a standalone building which served as a majlis. I had also heard stories about how the founder and first president of the UAE, Sheikh Zayed bin Sultan Al Nahyan, was known for having open majlis hours every week, where Emiratis could come to speak with him about their concerns for their country, about requests they might have, as well as ideas or suggestions they wanted to raise to his attention. This was a widely respected practice of Sheikh Zayed's and was explained to me as a traditional part of the Bedouin culture that many Emiratis in Abu Dhabi call their heritage.

"Please come with me," Qamar gestured for us to enter through the threshold. He guided us down a narrow hallway, and we stopped to greet his wife. "Can you please remove your shoes," he requested. We did and placed them neatly in the hallway. Qamar then guided us through a door into his majlis. Though I had never been invited into someone's personal majlis, I had sat on them at heritage festivals and fairs, and I had seen many vernacular historical photographs of Emirati men sitting on a majlis.

A few years earlier, I had commissioned the building of a small majlis-inspired couch for my first Abu Dhabi apartment. An Emirati friend took me to a majlis maker's shop in the downtown. Her father had his majlis made there and from the extensive books of material, samples of cushion firmness, and trims and design configurations, I got the sense that no one bought a majlis off the shelf but rather that the process of designing one from scratch was a part of owning one. My idea for a majlis at that time was a soft comfortable couch that used majlis fabric, design, and foam. Unfortunately, while the teal and brown striped material of my majlis made it a standout part of my living room, it was neither comfortable, nor a majlis, and I ended up selling it off shortly thereafter.

Robin and I walked into the majlis. I tried to take it all in without looking as though I was. Robin walked toward the back wall and sat, I followed and sat near him on the same long couch. Qamar walked out of the majlis, closing the door behind him to keep the air conditioning in. We both sat taking in the room, which from the inside looked nothing like the reflective glass façade.

Qamar's majlis was a large rectangular room with majlis couches lining three of the four walls. The fourth wall served as a place for the LCD television to hang. His majlis was beautiful, the couches were slightly short in their height with small golden legs, and a textured golden trim of roses and vines that ornately lined the bottom front of each. In majlis fashion, the couches were designed modularly to fit together along the length of a wall. The seat backs had striped fabric and a plush rounded teal cushion that provided most of the upper back and shoulder support. The teal material was pulled over the cushion using button tufting, creating plush pillow sections for the seat back. To my eyes, this effect made each section look like a couch for a queen.

The tile floor was covered by two very large beautiful silk carpets that looked like replicas of one another. They were both bright teal and sandy brown, with a central circular emblem and matching heavy border. The teals and browns in the carpet very closely matched the teals and browns in the majlis couches, which made me think the carpets were purchased first and the couches were designed to match. The walls were decorated from the floor to the ceiling with the same striped material used in the making of the majlis couches. The stripes ran vertically across the walls, appearing seamless, better than expertly hung wallpaper. A foot away from where the walls met the ceiling, a piece of dark brown fabric hung down in a ripple formation with several inches of gold tassel dangling from it. The ceiling panels were also covered in a fabric. These panels met at the top of the majlis where a rectangular built-in chandelier platform sat. The platform was covered in the same brown material with gold tassel hanging down around the edges. There were small tables scattered throughout the room, their surfaces covered with intricately designed teal and gold table covers that matched the room décor, upon which Emirati coffee pots, cups, and serving trays sat.

Robin looked at me with a big smile on his face and said, "Wow, this is amazing." "Yes," I responded. He was holding his spiral-bound notebook and a pen in his hand, the one he had brought to jot down notes for his book. Qamar entered the room, his daughter following behind, and sat on the majlis couch on the adjacent wall.

"So what do you think of my majlis," he asked.

Robin piped up. "It is amazing and very beautiful."

"So," Qamar asked looking at Robin's notebook. "Are you a reporter? Writing for a paper?"

"No, I am a writer, I write books," Robin responded. "I am writing a book on places like Madha that are parts of one country inside of another country. I would love to hear more about Madha."

Qamar began telling us about the history of what he called the Al Madhani, or the people who are defined by their connection to and inhabitance of Madha. He highlighted the families who had lived there for generations. He focused primarily on his own family whose roots in Madha go back a long way, and who have branches in Kuwait, Saudi Arabia, Syria, Palestine, Yemen, and Iraq in addition to Oman and the UAE. Qamar's English was very basic, but his interest in communicating was very strong. He told us that he was the owner of a sweets shop as was his father before him.

Qamar's wife is Emirati from Fujairah, and she works as a teacher in the nearby city of Khor Fukkan. However, he and his children are of Omani nationality, as citizenship in both countries is based on the father's nationality. Qamar went on to speak about his feelings and experiences about Madha, and the complexity of the exclave's relationship to the UAE. For example, while his wife can take advantage of free medical services in the UAE as an Emirati, he and his children must pay for medical services in the Emirates or travel the distance to the nearest Omani hospital, 400 kilometers away.

"Do you understand Nahwa?" Qamar asked.

"Yes, we drove through Nahwa today," Robin replied. "We noticed that they have a medical center there, and a school."

"Before, the people from Nahwa worked for my grandfather," Qamar said. "Whenever the Nahwa people needed to eat, they will come to work for my grandfather, and he would feed them. Now Nahwa has too much money, and Madha has nothing," Qamar replied.

"Before, Oman had a lot of money," I acknowledged.

"Yes, before, Madha had a lot of money." Qamar responded. "Oman had enough for all people to eat. Before if you had a UAE Passport from Sharjah or Fujairah, or Khor Fukkan, everyone would come and eat in Madha, but now everyone from Madha goes and works in Fujairah."

"So, people in Madha now work outside of Madha?" Robin asked.

"Now, yes," replied Qamar.

While we were talking, Qamar's wife and their helper came into the majlis and pushed a number of the small tables together placing a piece of plastic on top of the now larger table. They carried in serving plates, and then one serving dish after the next with food. There was a huge plate of rice, a bowl of cooked spinach, a bowl of salad, and a large bowl of chicken curry that sat on a metal frame with a small tealight below to keep it warm. On one far end of the table was a large bowl of fruit including strawberries, rambutan, and mangosteen, and at the other far end was a glass-covered dish of sweets, which I imagined were from Qamar's shop. In front of Robin and myself, they had placed a beautiful dish of three small bowls joined together in a line. In each bowl, there was half of a lemon. Qamar introduced the meal, "Tonight we did not prepare a special dinner as we did not know you would be coming, but it is just a normal dinner."

We thanked him profusely and asked him to join us. As is customary hospitality in the region and from my experiences, the hosts will often only eat after their guests. Both Qamar and his six-year-old daughter served us food and sat talking with us while we ate. Despite several requests that they please join us, Robin and I concluded our meal as we began, just the two of us with plates in hand.

"Rain," said Qamar.
"Is it raining?" Robin asked.
"Did you hear the thunder?" I remarked
"Inshallah it will come now," Qamar said.
"Excuse me Qamar, can I have my picture with you?" asked Robin.
"Yes yes, come come," said Qamar. "Where do you need picture?"
"I don't know, is this okay?" Robin asked.

Robin and Qamar sat on one of the long couches, and I snapped their photograph with both Qamar's phone and with Robin's. Qamar's wife entered the majlis, and we both said hello and thanked her for the delicious food. Her English was excellent, much better than Qamar's. She apologized for not preparing any traditional foods for us on our visit.

"You came from Abu Dhabi?" she asked.
"They came from Saadiyat," Qamar piped in.
"Did you go to Dibba?" she asked
"No, no," said Qamar.
"We only came here to Madha," I responded.

The television had been on in the background since we entered the majlis, the program loudly beaming into the room as we chatted with Qamar's wife about her being a teacher, about Saadiyat Island where I lived, about Nahwa, and about the places we had been on our trip.

"I will come back in December for National Day," said Robin. "Is it okay Qamar if I call you on your mobile when I am back?"

"Yes sure," said Qamar. Qamar passed his business card to Robin.

"You have four numbers," said Robin.
"I have three mobiles, for my business," he said.
"For National Day is there a very big celebration here?" Robin asked.
"Not here," said Qamar's wife, "In Nahwa. Nahwa has a huge celebration on National Day."

"Where are you from?" she asked Robin.
"I live in Singapore," Robin said.
"In Singapore? Nice, Singapore," said Qamar's wife.
"Have you been to Singapore?" asked Robin.
"No, my sister goes there," she replied.
"Will you come to Singapore?" asked Robin.
"What?" Qamar chimed in.
"Let me know when you come to Singapore," Robin replied.
"Bas too much expensive," said Qamar.
"Yes, it is so expensive in Singapore," Robin agreed.
"Expensive!" Qamar's wife proclaimed.
"Yes, it is expensive," I agreed.
"It is the world's most expensive city," said Robin.

We were at this point jiving in our conversation, managing to have one conversation while all speaking somewhat over one another.

"You live in Singapore?" asked Qamar.
"Yes, I do," said Robin.
"You work?" asked Qamar.
"I teach at a university," Robin replied.
"Which school, primary, secondary?" asked Qamar's wife.
"University," I said.
"University," she proclaimed. "Mashallah, very good," she said.

"So do you have many visitors coming through Madha?" I asked.
"Yes too much," Qamar's wife explained. "This season they come. Too much come from UAE," she said.
"Also from Kuwait," said Qamar.

"Why didn't I have to show my passport when I came into Madha?" Robin asked.
"Here, no they don't have any passport station here. There is no airport here, they don't have anything so nothing. But sometimes the police station makes a check

for someone coming here. Because some children 13 or 14 don't have a license ID card and they come here driving," Qamar's wife explained. "But it is too much quiet and safe here. Too much quiet."

They offered us sweets and dates and coffee. We discussed the food that Qamar's wife had prepared. Robin inquired about the spices used in the chicken, and we were told it was an Arabic mix of spices from LuLu. Qamar and his wife discussed the spices from LuLu in Arabic, while I explained to Robin that LuLu was a chain of hypermarkets in the UAE. The television was now blasting the soccer game with commentary in Arabic, and Robin leaned over to ask me if it would be rude of him to request use of their washroom. I told Robin it would be no problem and leaned over to Qamar's wife. "Is there a toilet here he can use?" I quietly asked her while gesturing toward Robin.

"Yes, yes just there, you can use," she responded.

Robin left for the washroom. Qamar was focused on the game.

"What's the weather now in Abu Dhabi?" asked Qamar's wife as we sipped our Arabic coffee. "Two days before it was very cool," I replied. "Then yesterday it was a little warmer and then there was rain. Usually, this time of year it is very hot but this year it is not, it is too cool," I said.
"Yes," she said. "It is winter still. Saudi Arabia it is too much raining, too much wadi."
"Before in Yemen and Oman it was the same, there was too much rain and flooding," I added.
"Yes, yes and ice," she said laughing. "You are also American?" she asked quickly changing the subject.

"Yes, I am from America," I replied.
"Where in America?" she asked.
"I am from New York," I said.
"Oh yes New York, New York," she repeated.
"Your family didn't come here to visit?" she asked.
"Yes, they came once before but not now," I replied.
"America is a very big country," Qamar's wife proclaimed.
"Do you know any people there in the USA?" I asked.
"Yes, yes, his niece, she is studying there now doctorate in IT."

She turned and yelled in Qamar's direction; he was completely absorbed in the game. "Qamar, Maria majors in math in America? Ay wain? Louisiana?" she asked. Qamar mumbled in the background, "New York."

"Oh, does she like the US?" I asked.

"Maria is in America for six years," replied Qamar's wife. "She is married also and has four babies."

"Is she married to an American?" asked Robin, who had returned from the bathroom.

"No no, Emirates," she replied.

"Oh is her husband also studying there?" I asked.

"Yes studying Engineering," she replied.

"Do they come and visit often?" I asked.

"Yes for the holiday they come back," she replied.

Glasses clinked and the soccer game roared as the sonic backdrop in the majlis. Qamar's children were cheering on the game; Qamar was silently watching. "GOAL!!!!!" was announced in Arabic with the same excitement, tone, and tenor as the sports commentary I am familiar with in English.

"Salad, salad, you eat salad," Qamar's wife yelled after her son.

Robin leaned over to me and said, "I think we should go before it gets too dark out. And it is such a lovely family and a lovely home, we must be sure to thank them."

"It was such a pleasant surprise for us to have you and your husband be so gracious," Robin said.

"Yes, yes nice to see you," replied Qamar's wife.

"Last summer we travel in Europe, we go in Europe," said Qamar's wife.

"Oh really?" Robin replied.

"We went in four countries. In German in Munich, then we will go to Austria, after Austria we go to Switzerland, after Switzerland we go to France," she said.

"Oh nice which was your favorite?" Robin asked.

"Hmm?" she thought about it for a minute.

"What did you like best?" Robin restated the question.

"Ahh Switzerland and Austria because all green," she replied.

"What city in Switzerland?" Robin asked.

"Interlaken," she replied.

"Oh Interlaken," Robin replied, "that is a very interesting place."

Khalas, we heard the commentator say on the television. A goal was scored, and the fans on the television were roaring, goal was screamed on the television over and over in English. GOAL! GOAL! GOAL! GOAL!

"This visit to your home was the best part of my day," Robin announced as we stood to indicate our imminent departure.

"I think we need to go back to Abu Dhabi, before it gets too dark," I said to Qamar's wife.

"You have my number?" asked Qamar.

"Yes yes," said Robin, "I have your number."

"Call us," said Qamar's wife. "One two days before you come because we will make the sweets for you," she said.

"Thank you," I replied.

"I hope to see you in December," Robin said to Qamar.

"Inshallah," Qamar replied.

"Thank you Qamar," I said. "It was very nice to meet you."

"Yes thank you," Robin said. "It is a very nice place here."

"No have the traffic, no have problem," Qamar said.

"Yes, just peace."

"Do you mind if I take one more photo with you before I leave?" Robin asked Qamar.

"Yes sure," Qamar replied.

I snapped a photo of Robin and Qamar; we then walked to the car. I looked at my phone for the time.

"It is prayer time?" I said aloud. This was more a question to Qamar than a statement.

"Yes," he said.

"Where is the mosque?" I asked.

"There down the street," he said.

"Okay thank you," I said as we began walking away.

We got into the car parked at the curb. I glanced at the time on my phone.

"Robin, it is four minutes until the call to prayer, do you mind if we go to the mosque to record?" I asked.

"Yes, sure," Robin said.

Robin was driving, and we headed down the street in the direction Qamar pointed until we saw a mosque on the next block. We pulled into the parking lot and turned off the car engine. I got my audio recorder set up and placed the earbuds in my ears. I hit the record button and waited for the adhan.

The mosque was simple looking, some of the paint was peeling of the exterior, and there was a single minaret jutting out of the top. What struck

Figure 24.1   Masjid Mushayhitan, Madha, Oman.

me most about the experience recording the call to prayer in Madha was the setting. The mosque, like Madha itself, was a bit sleepy, empty, and clean. There wasn't a person around aside from me and Robin, and the entire place was surrounded by large brown and black rocky mountains. The landscape was breathtaking in a difficult-to-describe way.

The adhan began, and the muezzin's voice was sweet and very melodic, serving as a perfect complement to the windy mountain air, and the birds chirping away from the date palm leaves on which they sat (figure 24.1 and recording 27).

Recording #27   Masjid Mushayhitan, Madha, Oman—Asr Adhan.

Conclusion

In her book *Art Objects*, Jeanette Winterson tells us that art changes our capacity for feeling and human emotion, it opens our heart.[1] The intention of the call to prayer soundmap project is to challenge people's Islamophobic assumptions, their fears, socialization, and misinformation toward and about themselves and others based on an association with Islam. Using sound, the medium most intuitive to me, feels like a powerful way of capturing the call to prayer, an outward-facing representation of Islam that welcomes and reminds all to pray. The adhan, in all of its sonic nuance as I have heard through the years, makes me feel something. It made me feel fear that very first time I heard it in Dahab, Egypt when I dropped to the ground, and today when visiting mosques in Sydney, Australia I feel excited as the adhan represents the connected nature of Islam around the world. The adhan in both of those circumstances was the same adhan, the thing that changed was me, my orientation to Islam, and my openness to it. I agree with Winterson that art has the capacity to open people's hearts and to make them feel. It makes perfect sense to consider art as a tool for interrupting people's fear and Islamophobia. I have found that this works for me, so why not for others?

The ten-year research project of recording the call to prayer at mosques around the world has been as much an exploration of art and self through the call to prayer, as it has been about the sonic recitation of the adhan and first-encounter experiences with each of the Muslim communities visited. In addition to the primary research objective of capturing recordings of the adhan from around the world, I was initially preoccupied with better understanding the role field recordings play in capturing data of community, and how that data in the form of sound can influence a listener's understanding of a person, culture, or community they don't otherwise understand. I wanted to better understand how recordings of the adhan and the first-encounter narratives told through sonic memory impact readers and listeners who have not necessarily visited these same communities. What I have found is that the practice of recording the adhan has been transformative for my understanding of myself, and by way of that, my ability to better understand the varied Muslim communities I have visited, recorded in, and written about. This extends to my ability to share my research findings in this book and importantly, my ability to develop creative work where I can share what I have learned and use the changes I have undergone in my own process to try and impact the thinking of others.

I have found that the very act of recording the adhan, sharing them on the soundmap, and exhibiting the recordings has begun numerous conversations with people from all walks of life about Islam. Some have been interesting and engaging, while others difficult and awkward. However, all have foregrounded Islam and Muslim communities in conversation. Attendees of the Sonic Storyboard exhibitions have expressed varied reactions to the work, but all have revealed that the work was a conversation starter about Islam and that the entry point of sound was different from that of religion. For some, sound was a more accessible entry point, and for others, it was simply a new experience. My hope is that this book continues to offer an accessible entry point into Muslim communities and the call to prayer, one that does not require travel, or perhaps one that highlights that travel is not required to meet your Muslim neighbors.

Conducting this research has forced me to confront and challenge the misinformation I was taught about Islam, as well as the Islamophobic socialization and conditioning I was exposed to growing up where I did, when I did. I grew up understanding that Islam was synonymous with Arab, and therefore Arab with Islam, meaning that all Muslims are from the Arab world, and all Arabs are Muslim. This is, of course, not true and contributes to a lack of understanding about what Islam means globally and how people who are Muslim exist in the world. For starters, people from the Arab world are members of most if not all world religions. That is to say, there are Christian Arabs, Jewish Arabs, Muslim Arabs, Hindu Arabs, and Buddhist Arabs, among others. There are also Muslims who live beyond the borders of the Arab world, all over the globe—like the Lipka Tatars, my ancestors, who lived in Eastern Europe for 500 years and now call Brooklyn, New York, home.

I know now that there is a mosque in every community where I have lived. There is a mosque down the street from where I used to live in Brooklyn, one on the corner of the block where I lived in Abu Dhabi, one in my old neighborhood in Delhi, and just behind my housing complex in Singapore. There is a musalla, a room outside a mosque for holding prayer, in the building next to where I work in Sydney, and there is a mosque a half-mile from the house

Conclusion

I grew up in on Long Island as a child. But as a child I didn't understand that there were religions other than Judaism and Christianity, which seems surprising now that I understand that Islam is an Abrahamic religion—one of the top three alongside Judaism and Christianity—that acknowledges Abraham as the first prophet called to a covenant by God. And I have learned that Islamic teachings include learning the stories from both the Torah and the New Testament.

As someone who left my hometown and the country where I am from in my early twenties, I have been searching for a while for my own sense of identity and self. My explorations of other cultures through living and working in them have been a motivator for my research and the way I move in the world. Researching the call to prayer has been an unpacking of my own cultural history and identity, and more than that, it has been a way of connecting sound, my intuitive medium for understanding things in life, to my research. Sound, my intuitive way of understanding, has been connected to how I navigate different cultures and communities, and to how I understand myself and by extension my research.

The research that fills the pages of this book predated any inkling that I would enroll in a doctoral program and has extended well beyond completing my dissertation. This work was not conducted in pursuit of answering a question I was posing for philosophical or intellectual purposes nor to confirm any hypothesis I may have had about Islam and sound. This work was born out of an intrinsic motivation and interest in ways of looking into another community and connecting to that community through something within myself. This intrinsic motivation has guided me to visit mosques everywhere I travel, and to travel in order to visit Muslim communities. This motivation is not something I cultivate. Instead, it comes from the place inside of me that wants to bring my full self to where I go and what I do. It is within the parts of me that fear or don't always fit.

My Jewish upbringing and my Queer identity were just as much a part of me on that rooftop in Rajasthan as they were when I decided I would move to the UAE for work. In fact, these parts of who I am along with all of my other identities are the places from where I cultivate my touchpoints. Perhaps, being Jewish in the Gulf and attending clandestine Rosh Hashanah services in a private home with a Rabbi who flew in from New York, after identifying my religion as Buddhist on my work visa application, is precisely the touchpoint through which I gained access to Emirati culture. Or perhaps, it was all of that alongside my then-burgeoning understanding of my Muslim heritage. This may seem strange but living in the Emirates as a Jewish Queer person of Muslim heritage, without a public place of worship, the legal security to express my love, or meetups for folks of intersectional religious identities, meant I was living a sort of veiled life. One life in public and another in private.

Having a public and a private life, I learned, was very common in the Emirates. Meaning, privacy is prized in Emirati culture, and while there are many rules, which are at times enforced by cameras in public spaces, people's private homes and lives are respected. In a way I was living as my full self in the way others lived as their full selves in the Emirates, within their homes. This touchpoint, an understanding of how I fit within a place, a culture, and country governed by Sharia law—that seemed on the outside in conflict with who I was on the inside—was actually the window through which I could access the Emirates.

For my public life, I put on coverings when I left my apartment to walk out into Abu Dhabi City. My coverings took the form of wearing certain clothes, not cutting my hair a certain way, making modifications to the way I interacted with my girlfriend in public, and the curation of the information I shared and communicated with those I did not know. Essentially, my covering was to disguise my queerness and Jewishness from public gaze. This feeling of covering when going outside was already familiar to me from growing up Queer in the United States in the 1990s. I knew there were places I could show my queerness and places where I had to temper, disguise, or cover it up. At times this was for safety reasons but sometimes this was for reasons of fitting into a culture or community. Wearing these coverings in the Emirates allowed me to access a sense of belonging in a place where everyone dons a covering. It is possible that through the alienation of not being my full self all the time, I was able to access something deeper about the culture of the Emirates.

This way of understanding myself in the context of the places I visit, research, and live allows me to relate to a community and through this relation understand the bias I have within me and how it affects the way I see and understand the people I meet. In the research I do in cultures outside of the one in which I was raised, these touchpoints become critical in learning about communities, places, and cultures, as they allow me to first understand something about myself in these communities, after which I can begin to make sense of the communities themselves. Perhaps, we all wear coverings some of the time, and understanding our own coverings is part of the key to better understanding ourselves, and through that understanding, we may find the touchpoints for understanding others.

Endnotes

NOTE

1. Diana Chester, "Beyond the Azhan: Abu Dhabi's Cacophonous Soundscape," *Journal of Sonic Studies* 18, Materials of Sound II (2019).

CHAPTER 4

1. Toong Soon Lee, "Technology and the production of Islamic space: The call to prayer in Singapore." *Ethnomusicology* 43, no. 1 (1999), 86.
2. Ibid., 87.
3. Michael Sells, *Approaching the Qur'an: the early revelations* (Oregon: White Cloud Press, 2007), 162.
4. Ibid., 163.
5. Translation of the adhan taken from John L. Esposito, *What Everyone Needs to Know about Islam* (New York: Oxford University Press, 2011), 19.

CHAPTER 13

1. Pierre Schaeffer. (1983). *Traité des objets Musicaux* (Paris: Éditions du Seuil, 1966).
2. Michel Chion, *Guide des objets sonores: Pierre Schaeffer et la recherche musicale* (Paris: INA/Buchet-Chastel, 1983).
3. Michel Chion, *Audio-Vision: Sound on Screen* (New York: Columbia University Press, 1994), 25.
4. Ibid., 28.
5. Ibid., 29.

6. Chion, *Guide des objets sonores*, 11.
7. J. Martin Daughtry, *Listening to War: Sound, Music, Trauma, and Survival in Wartime Iraq* (New York: Oxford University Press, 2015), 19.
8. Ibid., 101.

CHAPTER 15

1. Matthew Goulish, *39 Microlectures: In Proximity of Performance* (London and New York: Routledge, 2000), 101.
2. Oliver Batchelor, "Blå partier vil forbyde bønnekald: Socialdemokratiet er 'enige på bundlinjen," *Danish Broadcasting Corporation*, June 24, 2020, https://www.dr.dk/nyheder/politik/blaa-partier-vil-forbyde-boennekald-socialdemokratiet-er-enige-paa-bundlinjen.

CHAPTER 16

1. Peter Dallow, "Representing creativeness: practice-based approaches to research in creative arts," *Art, Design and Communication in Higher Education* 2, no. 1 (2003): 40–66.
2. Florian Dombois, Claudia Mareis, Ute Meta Bauer and Michael Schwab, *Intellectual birdhouse: artistic practice as research* (London: Koenig Books, 2012).
3. Andrew J Eisenberg, "Islam, sound and space: Acoustemology and Muslim citizenship on the Kenyan coast," in *Music, sound and space: transformations of public and private experience*, ed. Georgina Born (New York: Cambridge University Press, 2013), 192.
4. Ibid.

CHAPTER 19

1. Jean-Paul Thibaud, "A sonic paradigm of urban ambiances," *Journal of Sonic Studies* 1 (2011): par 17.
2. Ibid., par 2.
3. Ibid., par 18.
4. Ibid., par 13.
5. Paul DeMarinis, "On sonic spaces," in *Sound: documents of contemporary art*, ed. Caleb Kelley (Cambridge: Whitechapel Gallery and MIT Press, 2011), 74.

CHAPTER 22

1. Jacques Attali, Fredric Jameson, Susan McClary, and Brian Massumi. *Noise: the political economy of music* (Minneapolis: University of Minnesota Press, 1985), 4.
2. Sarah Pink, Heather Horst, John Postill, Larissa Hjorth, Tania Lewis, and Jo Tacchi, *Digital ethnography: principles and practice*. (California: SAGE Publications, 2015), 1.

CONCLUSION

1. Jeanette Winterson, *Art objects: essays on ecstasy and effrontery* (London: Jonathan Cape, 1995).

Bibliography

Attali, Jacques, Fredric Jameson, Susan McClary, and Brian Massumi. *Noise: The Political Economy of Music*. Minneapolis: University of Minnesota Press, 1985.

Batchelor, Oliver. "Blå partier vil forbyde bønnekald: Socialdemokratiet er 'enige på bundlinjen." *Danish Broadcasting Corporation*. June 24, 2020. https://www.dr.dk/nyheder/politik/blaa-partier-vil-forbyde-boennekald-socialdemokratiet-er-enige-paa-bundlinjen.

Chester, Diana. "Beyond the Azhan: Abu Dhabi's Cacophonous Soundscape." *Journal of Sonic Studies* 18 (2019).

Chion, Michel. *Guide des objets sonores: Pierre Schaeffer et la recherche musicale*. Paris: INA/Buchet-Chastel, 1983.

Chion, Michel. *Audio-vision: sound on screen*. New York: Columbia University Press, 1994.

Dallow, Peter. "Representing creativeness: practice-based approaches to research in creative arts." *Art, Design and Communication in Higher Education* 2, no. 1 (2003): 40–66.

Daughtry, J. Martin. *Listening to war: sound, music, trauma, and survival in Wartime Iraq*. New York: Oxford University Press, 2015.

DeMarinis, Paul. "On sonic spaces." In *Sound: documents of contemporary art*, edited by Caleb Kelley, 73–75. Cambridge: Whitechapel Gallery and MIT Press, 2011.

Dombois, Florian, Claudia Mareis, Ute Meta Bauer and Michael Schwab. *Intellectual birdhouse: artistic practice as research*. London: Koenig Books, 2012.

Eisenberg, Andrew J. "Islam, sound and space: Acoustemology and Muslim citizenship on the Kenyan coast." In *Music, sound and space: transformations of public and private experience*, edited by Georgina Born, 186–202. New York: Cambridge University Press, 2013.

Esposito, John L. *What Everyone Needs to Know about Islam*. New York: Oxford University Press, 2011.

Goulish, Matthew. *39 Microlectures: In proximity of performance*. London and New York: Routledge, 2000.

Lee, Toong Soon. "Technology and the production of Islamic space: The call to prayer in Singapore." *Ethnomusicology* 43, no. 1 (1999): 86–100.

Pink, Sarah, Heather Horst, John Postill, Larissa Hjorth, Tania Lewis, and Jo Tacchi. *Digital ethnography: principles and practice*. California: SAGE Publications, 2015.

Russolo, Luigi. "The art of noises." In *Futurist Manifestos*, edited by Umbro Apollonio, 74. London: Thames and Hudson, 1973.

Schaeffer, Pierre. *Traité des objets Musicaux*. Paris: Éditions du Seuil, 1966.

Schaeffer, Pierre, Christine North, and John Dack. *Treatise on musical objects: an essay across disciplines*. California: University of California Press, 2017. http://www.jstor.org/stable/10.1525/j.ctt1qv5pqb.

Sells, Michael. *Approaching the Qur'an: the early revelations*. Oregon: White Cloud Press, 2007.

Thibaud, Jean-Paul. "A sonic paradigm of urban ambiances." *Journal of Sonic Studies* 1 (2011): 1.

Winterson, Jeanette. *Art Objects: essays on ecstasy and effrontery*. London: Jonathan Cape, 1995.

Index

abayas, 73, 95
Abu Dhabi, UAE, xvii–xviii, 2, 31, 83–84, 90–92, 150; bike riding in, 22–25; field recording in, 25–27, 126–27; mosque alarm clock in, 11–14, *13*; Old Fish Market in, 21–27; Ramadan in, 115–16; Sheikh Khalifa Mosque in, 21–23, *22*, *23*, 25; W2 Mosque in, 21, 24–27, *26*
Action Together Suncoast, 119–21, *120*
adhan, xviii, 1; in Bali, Indonesia, 71–75; in Bangalore, India, 133–37, *137*; in Brazil, 57–59, *58*; differences and nuances in sound of, 15–19, 123–27; at Ezhara Beach, India, 108–10; first time hearing, 10; in Iceland, 31–35; at Imam Ali Moskeen, 92–96, *96*; importance of, 16; insider perspective on, 149–51; at Islamic Society of Sarasota and Bradenton, 112–21, *118*; in Italy, 43–50; at Masjid Mushayhitan, Madha, Oman, 175–76, *176*; in Al-Masjid An-Nabawi, Medina, 150–51, *151*; at Masjid Sultan, Singapore, 158–61, *160*, *161*; mosque alarm clock, 11–14, *13*; in Myanmar, 61–66, *66*; in New Zealand, 51–54; purposes for recording, 55–56; quality of, 4; Qur'an and, 16–17; recitation style of, 16–17, *18*, 32, 97, 123–27; in Salah Al-Deens Mosque Near Mt. Nebo, Jordan, *152*, 152–53, *153*; from Sheikh Khalifa Mosque, 21–23, *22*, *23*, 25; Shiite, 17–19; sonic context of, 123–27; soundmap of, 2–5, 15–19, 31–32, 56–57, 147–49, 177–79; Sunni, 17, 19; versions of, 17–19. *See also* field recording
Adobe Youth Voices (AYV), 129, 132–33
Ahmed, Omer "Kashmir," 149–51
AIF. *See* American India Foundation
airport travel, 67–68
Akuafo Hall Mosque, *18*
alarm clock, mosque, 11–14, *13*
American India Foundation (AIF), 129, 130
American Mohammedan Society, xix
amplification systems, 124
"anti-mosque" law, 44–45
anti-Rohingya sentiment, 61
Approaching the Qur'an (Sells), 16
Arab Street, Singapore, 158–59
architecture, 45, 61–63, 93, 96, 112
Art Objects (Winterson), 177
arts-based research, 99–100
arts practice, 99–101, 139

Asr prayer time, 15
Attali, Jacques, 147
Australia, 52, 52–53, 53
AYV. See Adobe Youth Voices

Bali, Indonesia, 67–75
Bangalore, India, 46, 129–30; field recording in, 132–37, *137*; Masjid E Noor in, 133–37, *137*; music in, 130–31
Bangladesh, 61
bhajans, 131–32
bias, 8, 180; of Islam, 4, 127; sound and, 101
bike riding, 92, 93; in Abu Dhabi, UAE, 22–25
Birthright, 8
Blue Mosque, Istanbul, 97
bodily knowledge, 100, 126
body-sound connection, 77–80
border control, 8–9
Brazil, 57–59, *58*
brochures, 52–53, 141
Buddhists, 61

Cage, John, 37
call to prayer, xviii; Dhuhr, 15, 30, 71–73, *73*; documenting, 19; environment and, 78, 94–95; on Facebook, 57; as global soundscape, 2; insider perspective on, 149–51; iqama, 17, 73–74; for Jumu'ah Prayer, 38, 45, *50*, 113–18, *118*; muezzin and, 16, 17, 39–40, 73–74, 109–10, 123–24, 136, 150, 160–61; salah and, 15, 17, 149; soundmap of, 1–3, *3*, 15; as soundmark, 16; times, 15, 16, 38. *See also* adhan; field recording
camping, 84–85
carpets, 93–94
causal listening, 78
Centro Cultural Beneficente Islâmico do Ceará, Fortaleza, Brazil, 57–59, *58*
Chester, Diana, 34–35
Chion, Michel, 78

Christchurch, New Zealand, 51–54, *53*, *54*
Christianity, 179
Chulia Muslim Dargah Mosque, Myanmar, 62–66, *65*, *66*
clothing, 71–73, 136, 144; headscarves, 32, 39, 141; veil and, 179; women and, 32, 39, 95, 141, 180
Composition as Explanation (Stein), 139
Comunita Islamica Di Firenze E Toscana, 45
Copenhagen, Denmark: field recording in, 92–98; Imam Ali Moskeen in, 92–98, *96*; Kozara's reflections on, 97–98
couches, 168–69
creative research, 100, 126
cultural differences, 59
cultural framework, 154–55, 177–78
cultural heritage, 64, 168, 179
cultural identity, 179–80
cultural understanding, 177–79

Al Dabb'iya, UAE: description of, 85; field recording in, 83–88; Sheikh Mubarak bin Mohammed Mosque in, 86–88, *87*
Dahab, Egypt, 9–10
Dallow, Peter, 99–100
Dana Castle, Jordan, 80–82, *81*
Daughtry, J. Martin, 79
Demarinis, Paul, 126–27
Denmark, 92–98, *96*
Dhuhr, 15, 30, 71–73, *73*
digital ethnography, 151–52
discrimination, 61, 114
Dombois et al., 100
dress. *See* clothing
DSM microphones, 47–48

Egypt, 8–10
Eisenberg, Andrew, 100–101
Emirati, 163–72
emotion, 177
environment: call to prayer and, 78, 94–95; field recording and, 37–38,

40–41, 56, 78–80, 87, 108, 124–27; framing and, 55–56; sound and, 37–38, 79–80, 108, 124–25, 153; soundscape and, 101, 103, 126–27
ethics, 99, 143–44
ethnography, 5, 56, 99; cultural framework and, 154–55, 177–78; defining, 151–52; digital, 151–52; ethnographic positionality in, 151–55; field recording and, xix–xx, 143–44, 147–55; insider perspective and, 149–51; sonic frame and, 147–55
Ezhara Beach, India, 105–10, *109*, *110*

Facebook, 2–3, 56–57
Fajr prayer time, 15, 17
fasting, 116
Félag Múslima Á Íslandi, Iceland, 31–32, *33*
field recording, 1–3; in Abu Dhabi, UAE, 25–27, 126–27; by Ahmed, 149–51; analyzing, 147–48, 177–79; in Bali, Indonesia, 70–75; in Bangalore, India, 132–37, *137*; in Brazil, 57–59, *58*; in Christchurch, New Zealand, 51–54; in Copenhagen, Denmark, 92–98; in Al Dabb'iya, 83–88; as documentation, 19; DSM microphones and, 47–48; environment and, 37–38, 40–41, 56, 78–80, 87, 108, 124–27; equipment, 47–48, 155; ethnography and, xix–xx, 143–44, 147–55; in Ezhara Beach, India, 106–10, *110*; in Florence, Italy, 44–50; framing and, 55–56; intentions and motivations for, 62, 149, 179; in Jordan, 80–82, *81*, *148*, 148–49, *152*, 152–53, *153*; key factors regarding, 124; learning through, 56, 59, 177–80; listening to, 80–81, 178; memory and, 78–82; methods, 37–41; of Moslem Mosque Inc., xix–xx, *xx*; of mosque alarm clock, 12–13, *13*;
permission for, 152–53; planning, 38–39, 124; purposes for, 55–56; requirements for submitting, 4; in Reykjavik, Iceland, 30–35, 123–24; in Sarasota, Florida, 111–18, *118*; in Saudi Arabia, 150–51, *151*; scholarly art and, 99–103; setting up for, 30; in Singapore, 157–61; sonic context of, 123–27; in *Sonic Storyboard: A Call to Prayer* project, 102–3; in Stockholm, Sweden, 140–45, *145*; as translation, 55–59; in Yangon, Myanmar, 61–66, *66*
fire hydrant culture, 166
Fittja Grand Mosque, 139–40
Florence, Italy, 43–44; adhan in, 44–50; Imam in, 48–49; Masjid Al-Taqwa in, 45–50, *49*, *50*
Florida: Action Together Suncoast in, 119–21, *120*; Naples, 112–13; Sarasota, 111–21, *118*, *120*
food, 44, 63, 121, 158–59; fasting and, 116; in Madha, Oman, 170–71, 173
4'33" composition (Cage), 37
framing, 55–56. *See also* sonic frame
Fujairah, UAE, 111

Gallery 4211, 102
gender separation, 57–58, 72, 94
geography and sound, 123–27
Ghana, 2, *18*
Ghweifat Highway, UAE, 83–86
global soundscape, 2

Haka, 52–53
HDBs. *See* Housing and Development Board
headscarves, 32, 39, 141
Housing and Development Board (HDBs), 158
Hindus, xvii, 74–75, 135
home, soundmap of, 2
horn honking, 154
human condition, 100

human connection, 59
Husserl, Edmund, 77

IAC. *See* Inter Arts Center
Iceland: adhan in, 31–35; Félag Múslima Á Íslandi, 31–32, *33*; Reykjavik, 29–35, 123–24
identity: cultural, 179–80; Jewish, xvii–xix, 8, 135, 179; Muslim, 64, 135; Queer, 179–80; religious, xvii–xix, 8, 64, 74–75, 135, 158, 161, 179; self, xiii–xix, 179–80
Imam, 16; in Florence, Italy, 48–49; Malik, 31–34, 123–24; in Reykjavik, Iceland, 31–34, 123–24
Imam Ali Moskeen, Copenhagen, Denmark, 92–98, *96*
India, xvii, 68, 89–90; Bangalore, 46, 129–37, *137*; Ezhara Beach in, 105–10, *109*, *110*; horn honking in, 154; musical systems in, 130–31
Indonesia: Bali, 67–75; Islam in, 69–75; Java, 75; religious identity in, 74–75
insider perspective, 149–51
interactive media technology, 100
Inter Arts Center (IAC), 103
iqama, 17, 73–74, 150
Iranian Mosque, 93–96
Isha'a prayer time, 15
Islam, xx–xxi; in Australia, 52; bias of, 4, 127; in Brazil, 57–59; in Denmark, 92–98; in Indonesia, 69–75; in Italy, 44–45, 47; learning about, 40, 52, 177–79; loudspeaker in, 15–16; in Myanmar, 61–66; in New York City, 115–16; in New Zealand, 51–54; salah in, 15, 17, 149; sound of, 15, 31. *See also* adhan; call to prayer
"Islam, Sound and Space" (Eisenberg), 100–101
Islamic Center of Naples, 112–13
Islamic representations, 123–27, 177

Islamic Society of Sarasota and Bradenton, United States, 111–21, *118*
Islamic Tartil readings, xvii
Islamiska Förbundet Stockholms Moské, Stockholm, Sweden, 140–45, *145*
Islamophobia, 1, 31, 53, 114, 177; misinformation and, 178; stereotyping and, 34–35
Israel, xviii, 8
Istanbul, Turkey, 97
Italy: Florence, 43–50, *49*, *50*; Islam in, 44–45, 47; Lombardy, 44–45

Java, Indonesia, 75
Jebel Akhdar Mountain, 4–5
Jewish Christmas tradition, 111–12
Jewish identity, xvii–xix, 8, 135, 179
Jewish temples, 73
Jordan: field recording in, 80–82, *81*, *148*, 148–49, *152*, 152–53, *153*; King Hussein Mosque, Amman, *148*, 148–49; Masjid Talha bin Obaidullah, 80–81, *81*; Salah Al-Deens Mosque Near Mt. Nebo in, *152*, 152–53, *153*
Judaism, 179
Jumu'ah Prayer, 38, 45, *50*, 113–18, *118*

Kannadigas, 135
Keezhara, Dhanaraj, 105
Kenya, 100–101
King Hussein Mosque, Amman, Jordan, *148*, 148–49
Kozara, Kasey, 89–96; reflections of, 97–98

law, 62; "anti-mosque," 44–45; Muslim Travel Ban and, 114, 119–21; Sharia, 180
Linköping University, 139
Lipka Tatar community, xix
listening, 149; approaches to, 77–78; causal, 78; to field recording, 80–81, 178; modes of, 78; reduced, 78; semantic, 78; sound and, 37, 77–78

Listening to War (Daughtry), 79
Lombardy, Italy, 44–45
loudspeaker, 15–16. *See also* adhan

Madha, Oman: food in, 170–73; history of, 169–70; Qamar's house in, 167–75; visiting, 163–76
Masjid Mushayhitan, Madha, Oman 175–76, *176*
Maghreb prayer time, 15
majlis, 168–69
Malaysia, 161
Malaysians, 158
Malik, Ismaeel (Imam), 31–34, 123–24
Malmo, Sweden, 103
mandir, 130, 131
Māori cultural dance, 52–53
Masjid, 69–70, 150–51
Masjid Al-Taqwa, Florence, Italy, 45–50, *49, 50*
Al-Masjid An-Nabawi, Medina, Kingdom of Saudi Arabia, 150–51, *151*
Masjid As-Sunnah An-Nabawiyyah Mosque, Pennsylvania, 39–40, *40*
Masjid E Noor, Bangalore, India, 133–37, *137*
Masjid Sultan, Singapore, 158–61, *160, 161*
Masjid Tentera Diraja, Singapore, 157
Max, visual programming tool, 102–3
Mecca, 15, 16, 32
medical services, 170
Medina, Kingdom of Saudi Arabia, 150–51, *151*
memory: field recording and, 78–82; sound as, 4–5, 10, 77–82, 153–54
Menezes, Guilherme, 56–59, *58*
mihrab, 71–72, 94, 144
misinformation, 178
modes of listening, 78
Mombasa, Kenya, 100–101
Morocco, 16, *17*
Moslem Mosque Inc., xix–xx, *xx*

mosque alarm clock, 11–14, *13*
Mosque Jebel Akhdar, Oman, 4–5, *5*
mosques: "anti-mosque" law and, 44–45; gender separation in, 57–58, 72, 94; permission for recording in, 152–53. *See also* adhan; field recording; *specific mosques*
Mount Holyoke College, 89–90
muezzin, 39–40, 73–74, 109–10, 136, 150, 160–61; recitation style and, 16–17, *18*, 32, 97, 123–27
musallah, 178
Mushollah Ubudiyah, 69
musical systems, 130–31
Muslim identity, 64, 135
Muslim stereotyping, 34–35
Muslim Travel Ban, 114, 119–21
Myanmar, 61–66, *65, 66*

Nahwa, Emirati enclave, 163–72
Naples, Florida, 112–13
New York City, New York, xix, 2, 44, 47, 67, 111–12, 132, 173; fire hydrant culture in, 166; horn honking in, 154; Islam in, 115–16; Moslem Mosque Inc., in, xix–xx, *xx*; September 11, 2001, in, xviii, 89–92, 114
New Zealand, 51–54, *53, 54*
NGOs. *See* nongovernmental organizations
Nicaragua, 7–8
9/11. *See* September 11, 2001
noise, 147
Noise (Attali), 147
nongovernmental organizations (NGOs), 61, 129
Al Noor Mosque, Christchurch, New Zealand, 51–54, *53, 54*

Old Fish Market, Abu Dhabi, UAE, 21–27
Oman: Madha, 163–76; Mosque Jebel Akhdar in, 4–5, *5*
"On Sonic Spaces" (Demarinis), 126–27

pamphlets, 52–53, 141
Pennsylvania, United States, 39–40
perceiving sound, 125–26
permission, 152–53
Perth Mosque, Australia, *52*, 52–53, *53*
phenomenology, 77
piano, 43–44
Pink, Sarah, 151
Pink et al., 151–52
politics, 8, 97, 114, 130
prayer: salat, 15, 17, 149; times, 15, 16, 38. *See also* call to prayer
private life, 179–80
protests, 114, 118–21, *120*
public life, 179–80

Queer identity, 179–80
Qur'an, xvii, 52, 150; adhan and, 16–17

racism, 61, 114
ragas, 131
Rajajinagar house, 130–32
Ramadan, 32, 33–34, 111; in Abu Dhabi, UAE, 115–16; fasting during, 116
recitation style, 16–17, *18*, 32, 97, 123–27
reduced listening, 78
refugees, 114
religion. *See specific religions*
religious celebrations, 111–12, 115–16. *See also* Ramadan
religious conversion, 59
religious identity, xvii–xix, 8, 64, 74–75, 135, 158, 161, 179
representations, of Islam, 123–27, 177
research, xix–xxi; arts-based, 99–100; creative, 100, 126; scientific methods and, 99–100
Reykjavik, Iceland: field recording in, 30–35, 123–24; mosques in, 30–35; University of Iceland in, 29–30
rickshaw, 108
Rohingya, 61
Russolo, Luigi, 147

Salah Al-Deens Mosque Near Mt. Nebo, Jordan, *152*, 152–53, *153*
salah worship, 15, 17, 143–44, 149, 151
Sandinista Revolutionaries, 7–8
Sarasota, Florida: field recording in, 111–18, *118*; Islamic Society of Sarasota and Bradenton in, 111–21, *118*; protests in, 114, 118–21, *120*
Sa Re Ga Ma musical system, 131
Sathya Sai Baba, 130, 131
Saudi Arabia, 150–51, *151*
Schaeffer, Pierre, 77–78
scholarly art, 99–103
scientific methods, 99–100
self-identity, xiii–xix, 179–80
Sells, Michael, 16
semantic listening, 78
sensing sound, 125–26
September 11, 2001, xviii, 89–92, 114
Sharia Law, 180
Sheikh Khalifa Mosque, 21–23, *22*, *23*, 25
Sheikh Mubarak bin Mohammed Mosque, Al Dabb'iya, 86–88, *87*
Shiite adhan, 17–19
shootings, 51
Singapore, 105, 125, 157–61, 163, 172
sitar, 131
social media, 2–3, 56–57
sonic context, 123–27
sonic frame, 56; ethnography and, 147–55
sonic quality, 124
Sonic Storyboard: A Call to Prayer project, 100–103
sound: amplification systems, 124; bias and, 101; body-sound connection, 77–80; data, 78–79, 102–3, 148, 153–54; design, 126–27; environment and, 37–38, 79–80, 108, 124–25, 153; geography and, 123–27; of Islam, 15, 31; Islamic representations and, 123–27, 177; listening and, 37, 77–78; as memory, 4–5, 10, 77–82, 153–54; noise and, 147; perceptions of, 37; sensing and perceiving, 125–26; sonic

context and, 123–27; sonic frame and, 56, 147–55; sonic quality and, 124; spacialized, 101; urban, 125
Sounding Islam exhibition, 3–4
soundmap: of adhan, 2–5, 15–19, 31–32, 56–57, 147–49, 177–79; of call to prayer, 1–3, *3*, 15; of home, 2
soundmapping, 1–5. *See also specific topics*
soundmark, 16
soundscape, 19, 99; environment and, 101, 103, 126–27; global, 2; in *Sonic Storyboard: A Call to Prayer* project, 101–2; sound design and, 126–27; visual art and, 101; visual programming and, 102–3
spacialized sound, 101
Stein, Gertrude, 139
stereotyping, 34–35
Stockholm, Sweden: field recording in, 140–45, *145*; Fittja Grand Mosque in, 139–40; Islamiska Förbundet Stockholms Moské in, 140–45, *145*; "Thinking through the Digital in Literature" conference in, 139
Sunni adhan, 17, 19
Swahili Muslim community, 100–101
Sweden: Inter Arts Center, Malmo, 103; Stockholm, 139–45

tajwīd recitation style, 17, *18*
tartīl recitation style, 17
technology: interactive media and, 100; recording equipment and, 47–48, 155; technological mediation and, 101; visual programming and, 102–3
Thibaud, Jean-Paul, 124–25
"Thinking through the Digital in Literature" conference, 139
Tightmarte Village, Morocco, 16, *17*
Toong Soon Lee, 15
Torah, xvii
Traité des Objects Musicaux (Schaeffer), 77–78
translation, 55–59

trauma, 79
Trump, Donald, 114
Turkey, 64, 97

UAE. *See* United Arab Emirates
Ubudiyah Foundation Building Musollah, 70–75, *72*, *73*
United Arab Emirates (UAE): Abu Dhabi, xvii–xviii, 2, 21–27, 31, 83–84, 90–92, 115–16, 126–27, 150; camping in, 84–85; cultural heritage in, 168; Al Dabb'iya, 83–88; Fujairah, 111; Madha, Oman, and, 163–76; public and private life in, 180
United States: American Mohammedan Society in, xix; Florida, 111–21, *118*, *120*; September 11, 2001, in, xviii, 89–92, 114. *See also* New York City, New York
University of Ghana, Legon, *18*
University of Iceland in Reykjavik, 29–30
urban sounds, 125

Varése, Edgard, 147
veil, 179. *See also* clothing
violence: shootings and, 51; trauma and, 79; war and, 79; in Yangon, Myanmar, 61–62
visual art, 101
visual programming, 102–3
volcanic eruption, 74–75

W2 Mosque, 21, 24–27, *26*
wadi, 165–66
war, 79
Western music, 131
William J. Clinton Fellowship, 129
Winterson, Jeanette, 177
women: clothing and, 32, 39, 95, 141, 180; gender separation and, 57–58, 72, 94; headscarves and, 32, 39, 141; veil and, 179
wood-carving factory, 74

Yangon, Myanmar, 61–66, *65*, *66*

About the Author

Sound studies scholar, media artist, and educator **Diana Chester** uses field recording as the basis for exhibitions, compositions, and writing on culture, history, and the environment. Originally from New York and based in Sydney, Australia, *Sonic Encounters: The Islamic Call to Prayer* is their first book.

www.ingramcontent.com/pod-product-compliance
Lightning Source LLC
Chambersburg PA
CBHW021849300426
44115CB00005B/75